The Ultimate Guide to Italy

From Alps to Apennines

David A. Davidson

Copyright © 2024 David A. Davidson

All rights reserved. No part of this book may be reproduced, distributed, or transmitted in any form or by any means, including photocopying, recording, or other electronic or mechanical methods, without the prior written permission of the copyright holder, except in the case of brief quotations embodied in critical reviews and certain other noncommercial uses permitted by copyright law

TABLE OF CONTENTS

Introduction

- Welcome to Italy

- Overview of the Alps and Apennines

- What to Expect from This Guide

Chapter 1: Getting Acquainted with Italy

- Italy at a Glance

- Geography and Climate Overview

- Brief History of Italy

- Cultural Overview: Language, Customs, and Etiquette

Chapter 2: Exploring Northern Italy: The Alps

- Discovering the Italian Alps

- Alpine Regions: Highlights and Attractions

  - Lombardy

  - Piedmont

  - Trentino-Alto Adige/Südtirol

  - Veneto

- Outdoor Adventures in the Alps: Hiking, Skiing, and More

- Alpine Cuisine: Culinary Delights of the North

Chapter 3: Venturing Through Central Italy: The Heartland

- Introduction to Central Italy

- Tuscany: Rolling Hills and Renaissance Cities

- Emilia-Romagna: Gastronomic Capital and Historic Towns

- Marche and Umbria: Hidden Gems of Central Italy

- The Apennines: Nature's Sanctuary and Scenic Drives

Chapter 4: Exploring Southern Italy: From Coastlines to Countrysides

- Discovering the Charms of Southern Italy

- Campania: Naples, Pompeii, and the Amalfi Coast

- Calabria: The Toe of Italy's Boot

- Puglia: The Heel of Italy's Boot

- Sicily: A Mediterranean Jewel

- Sardinia: Island Paradise in the Tyrrhenian Sea

Chapter 5: Immersing Yourself in Italian Culture

- Art and Architecture: Masterpieces Across Italy

- Culinary Traditions: From Pizza to Pasta

- Wine and Gastronomy: A Tour of Italian Flavors

- Festivals and Celebrations: Experiencing Italy's Vibrant Culture

- Italian Lifestyle: The Art of Dolce Far Niente (Sweet Idleness)

Chapter 6: Practical Travel Information

- Planning Your Trip: When to Go and What to Pack

- Transportation: Getting Around Italy

- Accommodation Options: From Luxury Hotels to Agriturismi

- Budgeting Tips and Money Matters

- Safety and Health Considerations

- Useful Phrases and Language Tips

Chapter 7: Insider Tips and Recommendations

- Off-the-Beaten-Path Destinations

- Hidden Gems and Local Favorites

- Must-Try Dishes and Restaurants

- Cultural Etiquette and Customs

- Sustainable Travel Practices

Conclusion

Bonus

- 3 budget-friendly restaurants in Italy

- Budget-friendly hotels in the top 3 cities

INTRODUCTION

- **Welcome to Italy**

Italy, a place famed for its rich history, lively culture, superb food, and magnificent scenery, welcomes you with open arms. From the snow-capped summits of the Alps in the north to the sun-drenched coasts of the Mediterranean in the south, Italy provides an unrivaled tapestry of experiences that capture the hearts and minds of tourists from across the world.

1. **Historical Legacy**: Italy's history spans back millennia, with remains of ancient civilizations dotting its terrain. From the powerful Roman Empire to the Renaissance era, Italy has been at the forefront of forging Western culture. Visitors are urged to tread in the footsteps of emperors, artists, and academics as they visit the country's abundance of historical monuments, including renowned structures such as the Colosseum, the Pantheon, and the ruins of Pompeii.

2. **Cultural Riches**: Italy's cultural legacy is as varied as it is deep. Each area has its own distinct customs, languages, and culinary specialties, providing tourists a complex tapestry of experiences. Whether relishing a creamy cappuccino in a crowded café in Rome, admiring works by Michelangelo and Leonardo da Vinci in Florence, or eating freshly-made pasta in a rustic trattoria in Tuscany, travelers are immersed in the eternal appeal of Italian culture.

3. **Scenic Beauty**: From the gorgeous countryside of Tuscany to the craggy coastline of the Amalfi Coast, Italy's natural landscapes are as varied as they are magnificent. The country's diverse terrain, ranging from mountains and lakes to vineyards and olive groves, offers a lovely background for outdoor excursions, picturesque drives, and leisurely strolls. Whether trekking in the Dolomites, boating along the Amalfi Coast, or lounging on the beaches of Lake Como, holidaymakers are exposed to breathtaking landscapes that evoke awe and wonder.

4. **Gastronomic Delights**: Italian food is known the world over for its simplicity, freshness, and deliciousness. From creamy risottos and substantial pastas to crispy pizzas and exquisite seafood, Italy's culinary offerings are a feast for the senses. Each area claims its unique culinary peculiarities, reflecting the local ingredients and culinary traditions. Whether indulging in a typical Neapolitan pizza in Naples, enjoying a luscious gelato in Florence, or eating freshly-caught seafood along the coast of Sicily, travelers are encouraged to embark on a gourmet adventure that thrills the taste and feeds the spirit.

5. **Warm Hospitality**: Italians are recognized for their warmth, hospitality, and enthusiasm for life. Visitors visiting Italy are greeted with real friendliness and a spirit of camaraderie that makes them feel perfectly at home. From the cordial greets of merchants to the vibrant chats of people in piazzas, tourists are accepted as part of the Italian family. Whether enjoying a dinner with newfound friends, learning the art of

Italian gestures, or just absorbing in the vivid ambiance of a local market, travelers are welcome to experience the warmth and friendliness that characterize the Italian way of life.

welcome to Italy, a place of timeless beauty, cultural wealth, and genuine friendliness. Whether discovering ancient ruins, relishing culinary delicacies, or just soaking in the gorgeous environment, tourists are urged to embark on a voyage of discovery and enjoyment that will leave them with memories to last a lifetime.

- Overview of the Alps and Apennines

Italy's landscape is characterized by two spectacular mountain ranges: the Alps in the north and the Apennines extending down the length of the Italian peninsula. These mountain ranges not only form the country's physical landscape but also play a key part in its cultural history, biodiversity, and outdoor recreational activities.

1. **The Alps**:

- Stretching over Italy's northern border, the Alps constitute a strong barrier between Italy and its neighboring nations. This spectacular mountain range is distinguished by snow-capped summits, glacial basins, and pure alpine lakes.
- The Italian Alps are home to some of the highest peaks in Europe, notably Monte Bianco (Mont Blanc), which straddles the border between Italy and France, and the Ortler, the highest mountain fully inside Italy.
- The Alps provide a multitude of outdoor recreational possibilities year-round, including skiing, snowboarding, hiking, mountaineering, and mountain biking. Popular ski resorts such as Courmayeur, Cortina d'Ampezzo, and Madonna di Campiglio draw winter sports lovers from throughout the world.
- In addition to its natural splendor, the Italian Alps are also home to picturesque alpine communities, ancient cities, and cultural treasures. Visitors may visit scenic cities like Bolzano, tucked in the heart of the

Dolomites, or Stresa, overlooking Lake Maggiore, and find a complex tapestry of customs, languages, and gastronomic pleasures.

2. **The Apennines**:

- Running like a spine along the heart of the Italian peninsula, the Apennine Mountains are a rough and diversified mountain range that runs from north to south for nearly 1,200 kilometers (750 miles).

- The Apennines are characterized by undulating hills, deep valleys, and beautiful woods, giving a dramatic contrast to the towering peaks of the Alps. While not as high as the Alps, the Apennines nonetheless reach spectacular heights, with peaks topping 2,000 meters (6,500 feet).

- The Apennines are home to a richness of biodiversity, with various ecosystems supporting a vast variety of plant and wildlife. National parks like as Gran Sasso e Monti della Laga in Abruzzo and Pollino in Calabria provide refuge for endangered species and give chances for wildlife observation and eco-tourism.

- In addition to their natural beauty, the Apennines are also rich in cultural legacy and history. Visitors may visit old hilltop cities like Assisi in Umbria, meander through medieval villages like San Gimignano in Tuscany, or travel along ancient Roman highways such as the Via Francigena, which covers the length of Italy from north to south.

- The Apennines provide a broad choice of outdoor activities for nature enthusiasts and adventure seekers, including hiking, cycling, horseback riding, and birding. Whether exploring secluded mountain routes, resting in thermal springs, or enjoying local cuisine at mountain rifugios, visitors to the Apennines are welcome to experience the beauty and solitude of Italy's lesser-known mountain region.

The Alps and Apennines are two of Italy's most famous and awe-inspiring natural features, providing tourists a multitude of options for outdoor activity, cultural discovery, and beautiful splendor. Whether skiing in the Alps, climbing in the

Apennines, or just appreciating the panoramic panoramas from a mountain summit, guests are welcome to immerse themselves in the timeless grandeur of Italy's mountainous areas.

- What to Expect from This Guide

Welcome to the ideal resource for experiencing Italy, from the breathtaking Alps in the north to the rough Apennines running down the length of the Italian peninsula. Authored by travel enthusiast and Italy lover, David A. Davidson, this thorough book is meant to be your invaluable companion as you begin on your Italian trip.

1. **Expert Insight and Local Knowledge**:
- Drawing on years of personal experience and thorough study, David A. Davidson delivers insider secrets, hidden jewels, and expert suggestions to help you make the most of your stay in Italy. From lesser-known hiking paths in the Dolomites to off-the-beaten-path agriturismos in

Tuscany, this handbook is rich with essential insights and local information that you won't find in conventional travel guides.

2. **Comprehensive Coverage of Italy's Regions**:
- This book covers every part of Italy, emphasizing the distinctive sights, cultural legacy, and gastronomic delicacies of each area. Whether you're intending to explore the art-filled alleys of Florence, indulge in gourmet food in Emilia-Romagna, or soak up the sun on the Amalfi Coast, you'll discover thorough information and practical guidance to help you organize your schedule and make the most of your time in each place.

3. **Detailed Itineraries and Travel Tips**:
- Whether you're a first-time visitor or a seasoned traveler, this book provides a range of recommended itineraries to fit every interest and travel style. From romantic vacations in Venice to family-friendly excursions in Sicily, each itinerary is thoughtfully created to highlight the best of what Italy has to offer. Additionally, you'll

receive practical travel suggestions on everything from transportation alternatives and lodging recommendations to dining etiquette and cultural norms, guaranteeing a seamless and delightful trip experience from start to finish.

4. **Insider Recommendations for Authentic Experiences**:

- One of the strengths of this book is its focus on real experiences that go beyond the tourist circuit. David A. Davidson discusses his favorite local haunts, hidden jewels, and cultural events, enabling you to immerse yourself in the authentic flavor of Italian living. Whether it's learning to make handmade pasta with a local chef, attending a traditional festival in a medieval town, or touring a lesser-known archeological site, you'll find a plethora of options to connect with the heart and soul of Italy.

5. **Inspiration for Future Adventures**:

- Beyond practical travel tips, this book also seeks to inspire and kindle your enthusiasm for future excursions in Italy. Through colorful descriptions, gorgeous imagery, and fascinating narrative, David A. Davidson provides a realistic picture of Italy's landscapes, culture, and traditions, stimulating your imagination and driving your desire to visit every part of this wonderful country.

"The Ultimate Guide to Italy: From Alps to Apennines" is more than simply a travel book - it's a portal to unique experiences, cultural discoveries, and lifetime memories in one of the world's most intriguing countries. Whether you're planning a short city break or an extensive road trip, let this book be your trusty friend as you start on your Italian adventure of a lifetime.

Chapter 1: Getting Acquainted with Italy

Italy, a country known for its rich history, vibrant culture, and stunning landscapes, offers travelers from around the world an enchanting array of experiences to explore. It is vital to familiarize yourself with the essence of Italy, encompassing its cultural depth and vibrant lifestyle, before embarking on your adventure through the country.

- **Italy at a Glance**

The country of Italy, which is sometimes referred to as the "Bel Paese" or "beautiful country," is a mesmerizing combination of ancient history, cultural riches, breathtaking scenery, and exceptional gastronomic pleasures. Italy, which sits in the middle of the Mediterranean Sea, is a country of contrasts. It is a place where contemporary wonders live with old ruins, and where history and creativity coexist. This article provides a detailed overview of Italy, providing a glance into the country's many regions, rich past, and lively culture:

1. **Italy's varied topography encompasses the following**:
- Positioned in southern Europe, Italy protrudes into the Mediterranean Sea resembling a boot. Its northern neighbors are France, Switzerland, Austria, and Slovenia.
- Its boundaries are shared with Slovenia. There are snow-capped mountains, undulating hills, lush plains, and scenic coastlines that are all part of the country's diversified topography. While the Apennine Mountains traverse the length of the Italian peninsula, the Alps are the dominant mountain range in the northern areas. Italy's coastline is vast, with the Tyrrhenian Sea to the west, the Adriatic Sea to the east, and the Ionian Sea to the south. The country's islands, especially Sicily and Sardinia, provide extra coastline beauty and cultural richness.

2. **Cultural Heritage**:

- Italy's cultural heritage is unique, spanning thousands of years of history and impacting civilizations across the globe. From the great Roman Empire to the Renaissance era, Italy has been a birthplace of art, architecture, and philosophy.
- Rome, the capital city, is a living museum of ancient culture, with prominent structures such as the Colosseum, the Roman Forum, and the Pantheon. The Vatican City, an autonomous city-state inside Rome, is home to St. Peter's Basilica and the Sistine Chapel.
- Florence, the cradle of the Renaissance, is famed for its richness of creative masterpieces, including Michelangelo's David, Botticelli's Birth of Venus, and Brunelleschi's Duomo.
- Venice, a city constructed on water, is famed for its canals, bridges, and great buildings. The city's annual Carnevale festival draws people from across the globe with its extravagant masks, costumes, and festivities.

3. **Culinary Excellence**:

- Italian food is known for its simplicity, freshness, and deliciousness. Each area claims its unique culinary peculiarities, reflecting the local ingredients and culinary traditions.
- Pasta, pizza, risotto, and gelato are just a handful of Italy's renowned meals, adored by residents and tourists alike. Olive oil, tomatoes, cheese, and wine are basic components in Italian cookery, adding to the country's gourmet renown.
- Italy's culinary culture is profoundly established in tradition, with meals considered a social and cultural event. From relaxing meals with family and friends to lively food markets and street festivals, food is a vital aspect of Italian culture.

4. **Warm Hospitality**:
- Italians are noted for their warmth, hospitality, and enthusiasm for life. Visitors to Italy are greeted with open arms and treated as valued guests, whether they're eating dinner in a family-run trattoria or starting up a chat with residents in a neighborhood cafe.

- Hospitality is a cornerstone of Italian culture, with customs such as the aperitivo, the afternoon practice of having beverages and food with friends, representing the spirit of conviviality and togetherness.

- Whether you're touring big cities or tiny towns, you'll discover that Italians take pleasure in sharing their history, tradition, and culinary delights with guests, ensuring that your trip in Italy is as memorable as it is genuine.

Italy is a nation of unsurpassed beauty, cultural richness, and great welcome. From the ancient ruins of Rome to the Renaissance treasures of Florence, from the romantic canals of Venice to the sun-drenched sands of the Amalfi Coast, Italy welcomes you to discover its different landscapes, experience its culinary pleasures, and immerse yourself in its timeless beauty.

- Geography and Climate Overview

Italy's geology and climate are as varied as they are compelling, allowing travelers a broad choice of landscapes and temperatures to explore. From the snow-capped summits of the Alps in the north to the sun-drenched beaches of the Mediterranean in the south, Italy's geographical variety is a monument to its rich natural heritage.

1. **Geography**:
- Italy is situated in southern Europe, surrounded by France, Switzerland, Austria, and Slovenia to the north. It is a peninsula stretching into the Mediterranean Sea, with the Tyrrhenian Sea to the west, the Adriatic Sea to the east, and the Ionian Sea to the south.
- The northern areas of Italy are dominated by the Alps, Europe's highest mountain range. The Italian Alps are distinguished by steep peaks, deep valleys, and scenic lakes, notably Lake Como, Lake Garda, and Lake Maggiore.

- Central Italy is home to undulating hills, lush plains, and ancient towns such as Rome, Florence, and Siena. The area is recognized for its vineyards, olive groves, and famous sites, including the Colosseum, the Duomo, and the Leaning Tower of Pisa.
- Southern Italy, often known as the Mezzogiorno, is characterized by a rough coastline, volcanic scenery, and ancient towns such as Naples, Palermo, and Bari. The area is home to notable sights such as Mount Vesuvius, the Amalfi Coast, and the island of Sicily.

2. **Climate**:
- Italy's climate varies widely from area to region, driven by its geographical variety and closeness to the Mediterranean Sea. Generally, the nation has a Mediterranean climate, typified by hot, dry summers and warm, rainy winters.
- Northern Italy has a continental climate, with hot summers and chilly winters. The Alps get substantial snowfall throughout the winter months, making them attractive locations for skiing and winter sports.

- Central Italy boasts a Mediterranean climate, with hot, dry summers and moderate, rainy winters. The area is noted for its nice weather year-round, making it a popular destination for travelers.
- Southern Italy has a Mediterranean climate, with hot, dry summers and moderate, rainy winters. The area enjoys warmer temperatures and less rainfall than the north, with long, bright days throughout the year.

3. **Regional Differences**:
- Despite its general Mediterranean climate, Italy displays substantial regional differences in temperature, precipitation, and weather patterns. Coastal locations tend to be milder and more temperate, whereas inland areas face more temperature extremes and changes.
- Mountainous locations, such as the Alps and the Apennines, receive colder temperatures and higher precipitation, especially in the winter months. The Alps are famed for their winter sports destinations, while the Apennines provide

chances for hiking, climbing, and outdoor adventure year-round. - Italy's islands, especially Sicily and Sardinia, have their own microclimates, with higher temperatures and less rainfall than the mainland. The islands are popular locations for beach vacations, water sports, and cultural tourism.

Italy's geography and climate provide a vast assortment of landscapes and climates to explore, from the snow-capped summits of the Alps to the sun-drenched beaches of the Mediterranean. Whether you're seeking adventure in the mountains, leisure by the sea, or cultural immersion in ancient towns, Italy welcomes you to experience its natural beauty and varied climate firsthand.

- **Brief History of Italy**

The history of Italy is a fascinating tapestry woven with threads of ancient civilizations, strong empires, artistic revolutions, and political upheavals. From the first inhabitants of ancient times to the modern-day republic, Italy's history is a tribute to the everlasting spirit and perseverance of its people. Here's a complete outline of the short history of Italy:

1. **Ancient Italy**:

- The history of Italy extends back to prehistoric periods, with traces of human occupation extending back to the Paleolithic epoch. The peninsula was home to several ancient civilizations, including the Etruscans, Greeks, and Phoenicians, who left behind remnants of their culture and influence.

- The establishment of the Roman Empire in the 1st century BCE turned Italy into a great hub of civilization, culture, and military force. Rome, established in 753 BCE, became the seat of a huge empire, reaching from Britain to the Middle East.

- The Romans made enormous contributions to architecture, engineering, law, and government, leaving behind renowned buildings such as the Colosseum, the Pantheon, and the Roman Forum.

2. **Medieval Italy**:

- Following the collapse of the Roman Empire in the 5th century CE, Italy experienced a period of political fragmentation and instability known as the Middle Ages. The Italian peninsula was split into various city-states, kingdoms, and duchies, each contending for power and influence.
- The medieval era witnessed the establishment of major city-states like Florence, Venice, and Milan, which became centers of trade, commerce, and cultural innovation. The Renaissance, a time of creative and intellectual renewal, started in Italy in the 14th century, ushering in a new age of innovation and humanism.
- Italian artists, philosophers, and intellectuals made enormous contributions to literature, philosophy, science, and the arts, creating the framework for the contemporary world.

3. **Rise of the Italian States**:
- The Italian Renaissance gave birth to the establishment of strong city-states and royal families, like the Medici of Florence, the

Sforza of Milan, and the Borgias of Rome. These governing families strove for power, resulting in a series of conflicts and warfare known as Italian warfare.

- The Italian Wars, which lasted from the late 15th century until the mid-16th century, saw Italy become a battlefield for European countries such as France, Spain, and the Holy Roman Empire. The conflicts ravaged the Italian peninsula, leading to economic collapse and political instability.

4. **Unification of Italy**:

- The 19th century saw the emergence of nationalism and the yearning for Italian unity, known as the Risorgimento. Led by individuals such as Giuseppe Garibaldi, Giuseppe Mazzini, and Count Camillo di Cavour, Italy went on a mission to integrate its numerous regions and city-states into a unified nation-state.

- The process of Italian unification culminated in 1861 with the formation of the Kingdom of Italy, under the authority of King Victor Emmanuel II of the House of Savoy. Rome, the eternal city, became the capital of the new monarchy in 1871, marking the end of the unification process.

5. **Modern Italy**:

- The 20th century brought tremendous political and social changes to Italy, notably the development of fascism under Benito Mussolini in the 1920s. Mussolini's fascist administration cooperated with Nazi Germany during World War II, culminating in Italy's defeat and occupation by cooperated forces.

- Following the war, Italy emerged as a democratic republic and became a founding member of the European Union in 1957. The post-war era witnessed unprecedented economic expansion and modernization, dubbed the "economic miracle," converting Italy into one of the world's top industrialized nations.

– Today, Italy is a flourishing democracy with a rich cultural legacy, robust economy, and varied culture. From its ancient ruins to its contemporary cities, Italy continues to grab the imagination of visitors and academics alike, exhibiting the ageless attraction of la dolce vita.

The history of Italy is a voyage through time, following the rise and fall of empires, the emergence of creative and intellectual movements, and the battle for unification and freedom. From its ancient beginnings to its modern-day republic, Italy's history is a tribute to the everlasting heritage of its people and the ageless beauty of its country.

- **Cultural Overview: Language, Customs, and Etiquette**

Language: Italian is the official language of Italy and is spoken by the majority of the people. It is a Romance language, derived from Latin, and is recognized for its musical tone and expressive gestures. While Italian is the predominant language, there are also various regional dialects spoken across the nation, representing Italy's broad cultural past. In addition to Italian, many Italians also speak English, particularly in tourist regions and major cities. However, it is always appreciated when guests make an attempt to speak simple Italian words, such as welcomes and expressions of thanks.

Customs and Etiquette: Italian culture lays a high focus on family, community, and tradition. Family relationships are crucial in Italian culture, with extended family members typically convening for meals, festivities, and religious festivals. Respect for elders and authoritative figures is also highly valued, with younger generations expected to defer to their elders in aspects of decision-making and social interaction.

When meeting someone for the first time, Italians often greet each other with a handshake and direct eye contact. It is traditional to use titles such as "Signore" (Mr.) and "Signora" (Mrs.) followed by the person's surname. Italians are recognized for their warm and expressive gestures, such as kissing on the cheeks or hugging, especially among friends and family members.

Dining etiquette is an essential component of Italian culture, with meals acting as a social and communal event. It is usual to wait for the host to ask you to sit down before taking your place at the table. Table manners are formal yet informal, with utensils used for eating pasta and main dishes, and bread used to wipe up sauce off the plate. It is considered disrespectful to begin eating before everyone is served or to leave the table before the meal is done.

In social contexts, Italians are noted for their vibrant talks and energetic gestures. It is customary for talks to be emotional and expressive, with interruptions and overlapping discourse regarded as natural. Interrupting someone while they are speaking is not always regarded as disrespectful but might be perceived as passionate engagement in the discourse.

Religion also plays a large influence in Italian culture, with the majority of the people identifying as Roman Catholic. Religious practices and traditions are followed across the nation, with festivals, processions, and religious holidays celebrated with enthusiasm and dedication.

Italian culture is characterized by warmth, friendliness, and a strong feeling of community. By observing local traditions and etiquette, tourists visiting Italy may completely immerse themselves in the rich fabric of Italian culture and build important relationships with the people they encounter along the way.

Chapter 2: Exploring Northern Italy: The Alps

Northern Italy is home to some of the most stunning and awe-inspiring scenery in Europe, characterized by the towering peaks of the Alps. From picturesque mountain communities to world-class ski resorts, the Alps offer a plethora of outdoor activities, cultural experiences, and beautiful landscapes for tourists to enjoy. Here's a thorough guide on touring Northern Italy and the Alps:

- **Discovering the Italian Alps**

Nestled in the northern regions of Italy, the Italian Alps provide a spectacular and awe-inspiring scenery that draws explorers, nature lovers, and cultural aficionados alike. From snow-capped peaks to green valleys, the Italian Alps offer a beautiful setting for exploration and discovery. Here's a thorough guide to exploring the Italian Alps:

1. **Alpine Landscapes**:

- The Italian Alps run over the northern border of Italy, establishing a natural barrier between Italy and its surrounding nations. This huge mountain range comprises a broad spectrum of sceneries, from towering peaks to verdant valleys and crystal-clear lakes.
- Among the most recognizable peaks in the Italian Alps are the magnificent Monte Rosa, the highest mountain in Italy, and the famed Matterhorn, recognized for its characteristic pyramid form. Other famous peaks are the Gran Paradiso, the Ortler, and the Dolomites, a UNESCO World Heritage Site famed for their stunning limestone formations.
- The Italian Alps are also home to various national parks and environmental reserves, including Gran Paradiso National Park, Stelvio National Park, and the Dolomiti Bellunesi National Park. These protected areas offer protection for a varied variety of flora and animals, as well as possibilities for hiking, wildlife watching, and eco-tourism.

2. **Outdoor Adventures**:

- The Italian Alps provide a multitude of outdoor activities for explorers of all ages and experience levels. In winter, the Alps become a paradise for snow sports aficionados, with world-class ski resorts such as Courmayeur, Cortina d'Ampezzo, and Madonna di Campiglio providing groomed slopes, powder-filled bowls, and adrenaline-pumping descents.
- In summer, the Alps come alive with a new type of adventure, as hikers, climbers, and mountain bikers take to the trails to explore the harsh terrain and stunning panoramas. From peaceful strolls through alpine meadows to demanding ascents of towering summits, the Italian Alps provide countless chances for outdoor adventure and discovery.
- Other popular sports in the Italian Alps include mountaineering, rock climbing, paragliding, and via ferrata, an exciting kind of climbing that includes crossing iron ropes and ladders connected to the rock face. Whether you're seeking adrenaline-fueled

thrills or quiet tranquility, the Italian Alps provide something for everyone.

3. **Cultural Heritage**:

- In addition to their natural splendor, the Italian Alps are also rich in cultural legacy and history. Throughout the area, travelers will encounter attractive alpine villages, historic cities, and cultural sites that represent the distinct traditions and customs of the mountain communities.

- One of the attractions of the Italian Alps is the rich local culture, which is celebrated via festivals, folk music, and traditional food. Visitors may savor substantial alpine cuisine such as polenta, speck, and fondue, or participate in the celebrations at events such as the Sagra dei Moccoli in Courmayeur or the Palio di Siena in the Dolomites.

- The Italian Alps are also home to a plethora of historical and architectural treasures, including medieval castles, Roman ruins, and gorgeous churches. Visitors may explore ancient cities such as Bolzano, Trento, and Aosta, or visit cultural institutions such as the Museum of

Archaeology in Trento or the Messner Mountain Museum in South Tyrol.

4. **Practical Considerations**:

- When arranging a journey to the Italian Alps, it's necessary to consider the time of year and weather conditions. Winters may be chilly and snowy, but summers are often pleasant and bright. Visitors should pack properly and be prepared for variations in weather, particularly at higher altitudes.

- Transportation options in the Italian Alps include trains, buses, and rental automobiles, as well as cable cars, funiculars, and chair lifts for reaching high places. It's recommended to verify schedules and plan routes in advance, particularly when going to isolated or rural places.

- Accommodation in the Italian Alps spans from luxury resorts and boutique hotels to quaint bed & breakfasts and mountain huts. Visitors may pick from a range of lodgings to fit their interests and budget, whether they're seeking a rustic mountain refuge or a sophisticated ski-in/ski-out resort.

Experiencing the Italian Alps is a voyage of exploration, adventure, and discovery, allowing tourists an opportunity to immerse themselves in the natural beauty, cultural history, and outdoor hobbies of this enchanting alpine area. Whether skiing in winter, hiking in summer, or just soaking in the beautiful scenery year-round, the Italian Alps guarantee a memorable experience that will have a lasting effect on those who come.

- **Alpine Regions: Highlights and Attractions**

Italy's Alpine regions are a treasure trove of natural beauty, outdoor experiences, and cultural legacy, providing travelers a broad selection of sites to discover. From magnificent peaks to gorgeous valleys, the Alpine regions of Italy capture the mind with their breathtaking scenery, charming communities, and rich history. Here's a detailed reference to the features and attractions of Italy's Alpine regions:

42

1. **The Dolomites**:
- Renowned for their spectacular limestone peaks, the Dolomites are a UNESCO World Heritage Site and one of Italy's most renowned Alpine attractions. Located in the northeastern section of the nation, the Dolomites provide spectacular landscapes, world-class trekking, and unrivaled outdoor activities.
- Highlights of the Dolomites include the Tre Cime di Lavaredo, a trio of towering peaks that are a symbol of the area, and the Sella Group, a large mountain massif famed for its beautiful rock formations and panoramic views.
- Outdoor lovers will discover a multitude of things to enjoy in the Dolomites, including hiking, mountain biking, rock climbing, and Via Ferrata. The area is also home to picturesque mountain communities like Cortina d'Ampezzo, Ortisei, and Canazei, where tourists may enjoy traditional mountain culture and hospitality.

2. **South Tyrol**:

- Located in the northernmost portion of Italy, South Tyrol is an area rich in history, culture, and natural beauty. The area is noted for its unusual combination of Italian and Austrian influences, evident in its food, architecture, and customs.
- Highlights of South Tyrol include the dynamic city of Bolzano, noted for its medieval Old Town, and the archeological museum containing Ötzi the Iceman, a mummified Neolithic hunter. The area is also home to the lovely towns of Merano, Brixen, and Bruneck, each having its own distinct attractions and atmosphere.
- Outdoor activities abound in South Tyrol, with chances for hiking, skiing, snowboarding, and climbing amid the region's spectacular alpine vistas. The Dolomiti Superski region, one of the biggest ski areas in the world, provides infinite kilometers of groomed slopes and contemporary lift facilities for winter sports aficionados.

3. **Aosta Valley**:

- Situated in the northwest corner of Italy, the Aosta Valley is a mountainous area recognized for its magnificent landscape, rich history, and cultural legacy. The area is home to some of the highest peaks in the Alps, including Mont Blanc, the Matterhorn, and Gran Paradiso.

- Highlights of the Aosta Valley include the ancient city of Aosta, famed for its well-preserved Roman remains, medieval architecture, and attractive cobblestone alleyways. The area is also home to various attractive mountain villages, including Courmayeur, Cogne, and La Thuile, each giving its own particular charm and attractions.

- Outdoor enthusiasts can discover a broad choice of activities to enjoy in the Aosta Valley, including skiing, snowboarding, hiking, mountain biking, and mountaineering. The area is particularly famous for its thermal baths and wellness facilities, where tourists may rest and revitalize among breathtaking mountain landscape.

4. **Trentino-Alto Adige**:

- Located in the northeastern section of Italy, Trentino-Alto Adige is an area recognized for its breathtaking alpine vistas, cultural variety, and outdoor experiences. The area is home to the Dolomites, a UNESCO World Heritage Site, as well as the gorgeous Lake Garda, Italy's biggest lake.

- Highlights of Trentino-Alto Adige include the picturesque city of Trento, famed for its medieval architecture, ancient squares, and thriving cultural scene. The area is also home to the lively resort town of Bolzano, where tourists can explore the Ötzi Museum, buy local crafts, and experience wonderful South Tyrolean cuisine.

- Outdoor activities abound in Trentino-Alto Adige, with options for skiing, snowboarding, hiking, mountain biking, and paragliding amid the region's spectacular mountain vistas. The area is also recognized for its magnificent hiking paths, such as the Alta Via 1 and Alta Via 2, which cross the Dolomites and give stunning views of the surrounding mountains.

5. **Cultural Experiences**:
- In addition to its natural beauty and outdoor activities, Italy's Alpine regions provide a plethora of cultural experiences and attractions for tourists to enjoy. From ancient castles and museums to traditional festivals and gastronomic pleasures, there's something for everyone to explore in the Alps.
- Cultural attractions of the Alpine regions include the castles of South Tyrol, such as Schloss Tirol and Castel Roncolo, which give intriguing insights into the region's medieval history and architecture. The area is also recognized for its traditional events, such as the Christmas markets in Bolzano and Merano, where tourists may enjoy the romance of the holiday season among festive decorations and seasonal sweets.

Italy's Alpine regions provide a multitude of features and attractions for tourists to discover, from beautiful alpine scenery to attractive towns, ancient cities, and cultural experiences. Whether you're seeking outdoor experiences, cultural immersion, or just a chance to rest among stunning scenery, the Italian Alps guarantee an extraordinary vacation that will have a lasting effect on everyone who comes.

- Lombardy

Lombardy, located in the northern section of Italy, is a region rich in history, culture, and economic importance. With its dynamic towns, stunning lakes, and lovely countryside, Lombardy offers travelers a broad selection of sites and experiences to enjoy. Here's a full examination of Lombardy:

1. **Geography and Landscape**:
- Lombardy is Italy's most populated and economically affluent region, surrounded by the Alps to the north and the Po River to the south. Its diversified terrain contains mountains, valleys, plains, and lakes, making it one of the most geographically varied areas in Italy.
- The area is home to numerous gorgeous lakes, including Lake Como, Lake Garda,

and Lake Maggiore, each giving its own distinct beauty and recreational activities. Lake Como, with its magnificent homes and attractive villages, is a favorite destination for celebrities and visitors alike, while Lake Garda is recognized for its crystal-clear waters and gorgeous cities.

- Lombardy's main city, Milan, is a worldwide powerhouse of fashion, finance, and culture, famed for its iconic buildings such as the Duomo di Milano, the Galleria Vittorio Emanuele II, and the Teatro alla Scala. Outside of Milan, Lombardy is filled with ancient cities, medieval castles, and gorgeous countryside, giving limitless chances for adventure and discovery.

2. **Cultural Legacy**:

- Lombardy offers a rich cultural legacy, molded by centuries of history and influences from numerous civilizations. The region's cities are home to an extraordinary variety of architectural treasures, including Roman ruins, Gothic cathedrals, Renaissance palaces, and Baroque churches.

- Milan, the city of Lombardy and Italy's

fashion capital, is a cultural powerhouse with world-class museums, galleries, and cultural institutions. Visitors may experience marvels of art and architecture at organizations such as the Pinacoteca di Brera, the Castello Sforzesco, and the Leonardo da Vinci Museum.
- Outside of Milan, Lombardy is home to many UNESCO World Heritage Sites, including the Church and Dominican Convent of Santa Maria delle Grazie with "The Last Supper" by Leonardo da Vinci, the Historic Center of Mantua, and the Prehistoric Pile dwellings surrounding the Alps.

3. **Cuisine and Gastronomy**:
- Lombardy's cuisine is a reflection of its diversified environment and strong agricultural tradition, with a concentration on fresh, seasonal ingredients and substantial, delicious meals. The area is noted for its risotto, polenta, ossobuco, and cotoletta alla Milanese, as well as its world-renowned cheeses like Gorgonzola, Taleggio, and Grana Padano.

- Milan, in particular, is a gastronomic hotspot with a thriving food scene that includes Michelin-starred restaurants, historic trattorias, and modern cafés. Visitors may try local specialties at lively food markets like the Mercato di Rialto and the Mercato di Porta Genova, or enjoy aperitivo, the Italian custom of pre-dinner beverages and nibbles, at one of the city's numerous stylish restaurants and cafes.

- Lombardy is also famed for its wines, with various wine-producing locations distributed around the province. The Oltrepò Pavese, Franciacorta, and Valtellina districts are famed for their high-quality wines, including sparkling wines, reds, and whites, which mix nicely with Lombardy's exquisite food.

4. **Outdoor Activities and Recreation**:
- Beyond its busy towns and cultural attractions, Lombardy provides a plethora of outdoor sports and leisure options for tourists to enjoy. The region's lakes, mountains, and countryside give the ideal setting for hiking, cycling, sailing, and skiing, depending on the season.

- Lake Como, Lake Garda, and Lake Maggiore are popular locations for water sports aficionados, providing chances for swimming, boating, windsurfing, and kiteboarding. The lakeside towns and villages also provide magnificent walking and cycling pathways, as well as gorgeous beaches and waterfront promenades.
- In the winter months, the Lombardy Alps become a paradise for snow sports fans, with world-class ski resorts such as Bormio, Livigno, and Madesimo providing groomed slopes, powder-filled bowls, and stunning mountain vistas. Visitors may also enjoy snowshoeing, cross-country skiing, and sledding in the region's stunning alpine vistas.

5. **Economic and Industrial Importance**:
- Lombardy is Italy's economic powerhouse, accounting for a large share of the country's GDP and industrial production. Milan, in particular, is a worldwide hub for finance, fashion, design, and manufacturing, with headquarters of multinational firms, luxury

brands, and fashion houses headquartered in the city.

- The area is also noted for its creativity and entrepreneurship, with a vibrant startup environment and research institutes in disciplines like technology, biotech, and renewable energy. Lombardy's economic prosperity has contributed to its lively and international climate, drawing talent and investment from throughout the globe.

Lombardy is an area of contrasts and tensions, where ancient history meets contemporary innovation, and urban sophistication coexists with natural beauty. From the busy streets of Milan to the peaceful beaches of Lake Como, Lombardy offers tourists a broad variety of experiences and sites to discover, making it a must-visit destination for travelers wishing to see the heart of northern Italy.

- **Piedmont**

Closed in the northwest corner of Italy, Piedmont (Piemonte in Italian) is a region of outstanding beauty, ancient history, and gastronomic brilliance. From the magnificent Alps to the undulating hills of the Langhe, Piedmont offers tourists a broad selection of sites and experiences to explore. Here's a full examination of Piedmont:

1. **Topography and Landscape**:
- Piedmont is defined by its diversified topography, which includes the high peaks of the Alps to the north, the rich plains of the Po River Valley, and the scenic hills of the Langhe and Monferrato areas to the south.
- The area is recognized for its magnificent natural beauty, with snow-capped mountains, verdant valleys, and vineyard-covered slopes offering a beautiful background for exploration and outdoor experiences.
- Piedmont is also home to numerous significant rivers, notably the Po, the longest river in Italy, which runs through the center of the area and offers rich soil for agriculture and vineyards.

2. **Cultural Legacy**:

- Piedmont possesses a rich cultural legacy, molded by centuries of history and influences from numerous civilizations. The region's cities and villages are filled with historic sites, UNESCO World Heritage Sites, and architectural marvels that represent its illustrious history.
- Turin, the capital of Piedmont, is a city of large boulevards, exquisite squares, and Baroque palaces, with attractions such as the Royal Palace of Turin, the Mole Antonelliana, and the Palazzo Madama. The city is also home to world-class museums, notably the Museo Egizio, one of the most significant Egyptian museums in the world.
- Outside of Turin, Piedmont is peppered with picturesque hilltop towns, ancient castles, and walled villages that provide insights into the region's medieval and Renaissance past. The Sacri Monti (Sacred Mountains) in Piedmont, a set of nine ecclesiastical complexes and chapels, are UNESCO World Heritage Sites and are famous for their architectural and cultural importance.

3. **Cuisine & Gastronomy**:
- Piedmont is widely described as the gastronomic center of Italy, owing to its rich culinary traditions, quality ingredients, and world-renowned dishes. The area is famed for its truffles, notably the treasured white truffles of Alba, which are regarded as some of the best in the world.
- Piedmont is also recognized for its wines, notably Barolo and Barbaresco, two of Italy's most prominent red wines, created from the Nebbiolo vine. Other prominent wines made in the area include Barbera, Dolcetto, and Moscato d'Asti.
- Piedmontese cuisine is defined by its simplicity, concentrating on fresh, seasonal ingredients and traditional cooking techniques. Signature dishes include Vitello tonnato (sliced veal with tuna sauce), agnolotti del plin (little, filled pasta bundles), and bagna cauda (a warm anchovy and garlic dip served with vegetables).

4. **Outdoor Activities and Recreation**:
- Piedmont's diversified terrain provides a multitude of outdoor activities and

recreational possibilities for tourists to enjoy. In the Alps, outdoor enthusiasts may explore hiking paths, mountain biking routes, and ski slopes, while in the Langhe and Monferrato areas, tourists can cycle through vineyards, trek along picturesque trails, and enjoy wine tastings at local wineries.

- The area is also home to numerous national parks and natural reserves, notably the Gran Paradiso National Park, Italy's oldest national park, which provides chances for animal observation, climbing, and alpine trekking.

- Piedmont's lakes, notably Lake Maggiore, Lake Orta, and Lake Viverone give extra chances for water activities including sailing, windsurfing, and kayaking, as well as relaxing boat rides and picnics along the coast.

5. **Economic and Industrial Importance**:

- Piedmont is a significant economic and industrial hub in Italy, with a broad economy that encompasses industry, agriculture, tourism, and technology. Turin, in particular, is recognized for its automobile sector, with Fiat Chrysler Automobiles (FCA) based in the city.

- The area is also home to various research organizations and universities, notably the Polytechnic University of Turin, which contribute to Piedmont's position as a center of innovation and technical development.
- Piedmont's agricultural sector is dominated by viticulture, with wine production playing a large part in the region's economy. The region's wines are exported across the globe and are a source of pride for Piedmontese growers and people alike.

Piedmont is an area of contrasts and paradoxes, where old traditions meet contemporary innovation, and natural beauty coexists with urban sophistication. Whether experiencing the ancient districts of Turin, tasting the delicacies of Piedmontese cuisine, or climbing through the vineyard-covered hills of the Langhe, Piedmont offers guests a genuinely memorable experience that will make a lasting impact on all who come.

- **Trentino-Alto Adige/Südtirol**

Closed in the northeastern corner of Italy, Trentino-Alto Adige/Südtirol is an area of spectacular natural beauty, rich cultural legacy, and distinctive linguistic and ethnic variety. Comprising two autonomous provinces, Trentino and South Tyrol (Alto Adige), this area is a compelling combination of Italian, Austrian, and Ladin traditions. Here's a full examination of Trentino-Alto Adige/Südtirol:

1. **Geography and Landscape**:
- Trentino-Alto Adige/Südtirol is defined by its spectacular mountain scenery, with the towering peaks of the Dolomites dominating the northern horizon and the rich valleys of the Adige River basin reaching to the south.
- The region's diversified terrain includes alpine meadows, rocky mountain peaks, crystal-clear lakes, and luscious vineyards, giving a rich tapestry of landscapes for tourists to explore.
- Notable natural attractions in Trentino-Alto Adige/Südtirol include the Dolomites, a

UNESCO World Heritage Site famed for their stunning limestone formations and picturesque hiking paths, and Lake Garda, Italy's biggest lake, which provides chances for sailing, windsurfing, and swimming.

2. Cultural Heritage:
- Trentino-Alto Adige/Südtirol is an area of cultural variety, influenced by millennia of history and influences from numerous civilizations. The area is home to three primary language groups: Italian, German, and Ladin, each with its own unique traditions, customs, and dialects.
- In South Tyrol, German is the prevalent language, reflecting the region's strong links to Austria and its historical association with the Austro-Hungarian Empire. The region's towns and villages are peppered with lovely Alpine architecture, including chalet-style residences, onion-domed churches, and walled castles.
- In Trentino, Italian is the predominant language, although the territory also has a considerable Germanic influence, notably in the northern valleys. The city of Trento, the

regional capital, is famed for its medieval architecture, ancient squares, and cultural events, notably the Trento Film Festival and the Christmas markets.

- Throughout Trentino-Alto Adige/Südtirol, tourists may discover a multitude of cultural attractions, including museums, galleries, and cultural events that reflect the region's unique past and character.

3. **Outdoor Activities and Recreation**:

- Trentino-Alto Adige/Südtirol is a paradise for outdoor lovers, with a large selection of activities to enjoy in every season. In winter, the region's ski resorts, notably Val Gardena, Val di Fassa, and Madonna di Campiglio, provide world-class skiing, snowboarding, and winter sports.

- In the summer months, the region's mountains become a playground for hiking, mountain biking, rock climbing, and paragliding, with hundreds of kilometers of paths and routes to explore. The Dolomites are especially popular for hiking, with paths ranging from casual strolls to demanding multi-day treks.

- The region's lakes, notably Lake Garda, Lake Braies, and Lake Caldaro provide chances for swimming, boating, and water sports, as well as lovely picnics and leisurely walks along the beach.

4. **Cuisine and Gastronomy**:
- Trentino-Alto Adige/Südtirol enjoys a rich culinary legacy that reflects its numerous cultural influences and bountiful natural resources. The area is noted for its robust mountain cuisine, which includes dishes such as canederli (bread dumplings), speck (smoked ham), and knödel (dumplings).
- South Tyrol is famed for its speck and Schlutzkrapfen (stuffed pasta), as well as its pastries and sweets, such as strudel and kaiserschmarrn (shredded pancake). Trentino, on the other hand, is famed for its freshwater fish dishes, including trout and char, as well as its apple-based sweets and wines.
- The region's wines, especially those from South Tyrol, are widely acclaimed for their quality and variety, with varieties such as

Lagrein, Gewürztraminer, and Schiava grown in the region's vineyards.

5. Economic and Industrial Importance:

- Trentino-Alto Adige/Südtirol has a varied economy that includes agriculture, tourism, manufacturing, and services. The region's steep topography and lush valleys support a vibrant agricultural industry, with wineries, orchards, and dairy farms providing a broad variety of goods.

- Tourism is a key sector in Trentino-Alto Adige/Südtirol, bringing millions of people each year to experience the region's natural beauty, outdoor activities, and cultural attractions. The region's ski resorts, spa towns, and historic cities are especially attractive destinations for travelers from throughout the globe.

- The area is also recognized for its manufacturing industry, with businesses focusing on fields such as automotive, equipment, and precision engineering. Trentino-Alto Adige/Südtirol has a rich legacy of craftsmanship and invention, with numerous local craftsmen making high-quality items like wood carvings, pottery, and textiles.

Trentino-Alto Adige/Südtirol is a region of breathtaking natural beauty, rich cultural legacy, and different customs, making it a genuinely unique destination within Italy. Whether exploring the magnificent peaks of the Dolomites, experiencing the aromas of Alpine cuisine, or immersing oneself in the region's multicultural past, visitors to Trentino-Alto Adige/Südtirol are bound to be fascinated by its beauty and attraction.

- **Veneto**

Veneto, situated in northeastern Italy, is a region of unsurpassed appeal, featuring a rich tapestry of history, culture, and natural beauties. From the renowned canals of Venice to the rolling hills of the Prosecco wine district, Veneto offers travelers a broad assortment of sites and experiences to explore. Here's a full overview of Veneto:

1. **Geography and Landscape**:

- Veneto is defined by its diversified geography, which includes coastal lowlands, lush plains, rolling hills, and steep mountains. The territory is bounded by the Adriatic Sea to the east, the Dolomites to the north, and the Po River to the south.
- The Venetian Lagoon, a UNESCO World Heritage Site, is a distinctive feature of the area, consisting of a network of marshy islands and saltwater lagoons that are home to the medieval city of Venice and numerous smaller islands.
- Inland, the terrain of Veneto is filled with attractive towns and villages, vineyards and olive groves, and old castles and palaces, giving a magnificent background for exploration and outdoor experiences.

2. **Cultural Heritage**:
- Veneto is immersed in history and cultural heritage, with a legacy that extends back thousands of years. The territory was previously home to the ancient Veneti people, who gave their name to the region and have been affected by different

civilizations, including the Romans, Byzantines, and Venetians.

- Venice, the gem of Veneto, is famed for its breathtaking architecture, art treasures, and charming waterways. Highlights of the city include St. Mark's Square, the Doge's Palace, the Rialto Bridge, and the Grand Canal, as well as world-class museums such as the Gallerie dell'Accademia and the Peggy Guggenheim Collection.

- Beyond Venice, Veneto is home to numerous more ancient cities and towns, including Verona, Padua, and Vicenza, each of which possesses its own distinctive attractions, such as the Arena di Verona, the Scrovegni Chapel, and the Palladian villas of the Veneto.

3. **Cuisine & Gastronomy**:

- Veneto is a gastronomic wonderland, noted for its fresh fish, savory risottos, and world-class wines. The region's cuisine is inspired by its closeness to the sea, as well as its lush plains and plentiful agricultural resources.

- Venice, in particular, is noted for its seafood delicacies, including sarde in saor (sweet and sour sardines), risotto al nero di sepia (black squid ink rice), and fritto misto (mixed fried shellfish). The city's cicchetti bars are also famous venues for tasting small dishes of local delicacies accompanied by a glass of wine.

- Inland, Veneto is noted for its substantial meat dishes, such as baccalà alla vicentina (salted cod stew), polenta e osei (polenta with tiny birds), and fegato alla veneziana (Venetian-style liver). The area is particularly famed for its wines, including Prosecco, Valpolicella, Soave, and Amarone, which are produced in vineyards dispersed across the countryside.

4. **Outdoor Activities and Recreation**:

- Veneto's diversified geography provides a multitude of outdoor activities and recreational options for guests to enjoy. Along the coast, tourists may swim, sunbathe, and sail in the blue waters of the Adriatic Sea, or explore the lovely fishing towns and coastal resorts that dot the coastline.

- Inland, the rolling hills and vineyards of the Veneto region offer the ideal scene for hiking, cycling, and wine-tasting trips. The Prosecco wine district, nestled in the hills north of Venice, provides gorgeous paths, lovely towns, and vineyard tours where tourists may enjoy Italy's most renowned sparkling wine.

- For outdoor enthusiasts, the Dolomites provide unlimited options for hiking, rock climbing, skiing, and snowboarding, with world-class ski resorts such as Cortina d'Ampezzo, Arabba, and Madonna di Campiglio drawing people from across the globe.

5. **Economic and Industrial Importance**:

- Veneto is one of Italy's richest and most economically vibrant regions, with a broad economy that encompasses industry, agriculture, tourism, and services. The area is home to numerous significant industrial hubs, including Venice, Padua, and Verona, which are noted for their manufacture of textiles, equipment, and consumer products.

- Tourism is a key economy in Veneto, with millions of people traveling to the area each year to enjoy its ancient cities, cultural attractions, and natural beauty. Venice alone draws millions of people yearly, making it one of the most visited cities in the world.

- Agriculture is also an important component of the Veneto economy, with the region's fertile plains and vineyard-covered slopes providing a diverse variety of commodities, including rice, maize, fruit, vegetables, and wine.

Veneto is a region of great beauty and cultural richness, where ancient history meets contemporary innovation, and urban sophistication coexists with natural majesty. From the timeless attraction of Venice's ancient canals to the scenic vineyards of the countryside, Veneto captivates tourists with its different landscapes, gastronomic pleasures, and timeless charm, making it a destination that really reflects the essence of Italy's cultural legacy.

- **Outdoor Adventures in the Alps: Hiking, Skiing, and More**

Italy's section of the Alps is a refuge for outdoor lovers, providing a broad selection of adrenaline sports among gorgeous natural settings. From peaceful treks through alpine meadows to exhilarating descents on world-class ski slopes, the Italian Alps present infinite options for adventure and discovery. Here's a full reference to outdoor experiences in the Italian Alps, including hiking, skiing, and more:

1. **Hiking**:
- The Italian Alps contain a huge network of hiking paths, providing something for hikers of all abilities. Whether you're a seasoned trekker or a casual walker, you'll discover paths that appeal to your ability level and interests.
- Popular hiking sites in the Italian Alps include the Dolomites, a UNESCO World Heritage Site famed for its spectacular peaks, rough terrain, and breathtaking panoramas. The Alta Via trails provide

multi-day walking expeditions through some of the most stunning scenery in the region.

- Along the journey, hikers may encounter lovely mountain communities, crystal-clear lakes, and lush alpine meadows overflowing with wildflowers. Wildlife lovers may also observe local animals such as chamois, ibex, and golden eagles as they explore the unspoiled wildness of the Alps.

2. **Skiing and Snowboarding**:

- In the winter months, the Italian Alps turn into a snowy paradise, drawing skiers and snowboarders from across the globe. With over 300 ski resorts dotted around the area, there's no lack of slopes to explore.

- Popular ski locations in the Italian Alps include Cortina d'Ampezzo, Madonna di Campiglio, and Alta Badia, each providing a distinct combination of terrain, snow conditions, and après-ski activities. The Dolomiti Superski region is one of the biggest ski domains in the world, with over 1,200 kilometers of linked slopes to explore.

- In addition to downhill skiing and snowboarding, the Italian Alps provide chances for cross-country skiing, snowshoeing, and ski touring. Adventurous skiers may also explore off-piste terrain and backcountry routes, finding secluded powder stashes and virgin snowfields with the support of professional guides.

3. **Mountaineering and Climbing**:
- For more experienced travelers, the Italian Alps offer some of the most renowned mountaineering and climbing routes in the world. From iconic ascents of peaks like the Matterhorn and Mont Blanc to difficult climbs on hard rock faces and frozen waterfalls, there's no lack of obstacles to conquer.
- The Gran Paradiso, the Monte Rosa Massif, and the Brenta Dolomites are just a few of the iconic peaks that lure mountaineers to test their abilities and stamina in the high mountains. Guided trips and climbing courses are provided for climbers wishing to improve their technique and face new difficulties.
- In addition to classic mountaineering, the Italian Alps provide a range of rock

climbing, ice climbing, and via ferrata routes for climbers of all abilities. The Dolomites, with their sheer limestone spires and exposed ridgelines, are especially known for their demanding climbs and breathtaking views.

4. **Mountain Biking**:

- In the summer months, the Italian Alps are a paradise for mountain bikers, with hundreds of kilometers of tracks and routes to explore. From flowing singletracks through alpine woods to challenging descents down rocky slopes, there's terrain to fit every rider's skill level and style.

- Popular mountain biking locations in the Italian Alps include the Aosta Valley, the Alta Badia area, and the Valtellina Valley, each having a network of trails and lift-accessed bike parks for riders to enjoy. The Dolomiti Lagorai Bike Trail and the Bike Transalp route are both popular possibilities for long-distance bikepacking adventures.

- Mountain bikers may pick from a choice of guided tours, self-guided rides, and multi-day trips, with possibilities for all-inclusive packages that include hotels, food, and bike rentals. Along the route, visitors may take in panoramic vistas of snow-capped peaks, stunning alpine lakes, and lovely mountain communities, making memories that last a lifetime.

5. **Paragliding and Hang Gliding**:
- For those wanting a bird's-eye perspective of the Italian Alps, paragliding and hang gliding provide a unique and exciting opportunity to explore the region's grandeur from above. Tandem flights are offered for novices, enabling them to fly far over the mountains while harnessed to an expert pilot.

- Popular paragliding sites in the Italian Alps include the Aosta Valley, Lake Garda, and the Brenta Dolomites, each providing great conditions for flying and stunning views of the surrounding scenery. Hang gliding fans may also find possibilities to take to the skies at authorized flying sites around the Alps.

- Paragliding and hang gliding trips normally take from 20 minutes to an hour, depending on weather conditions and pilot expertise. Participants may experience magnificent views of snow-capped peaks, green valleys, and picturesque mountain towns, generating memories of a lifetime and a renewed appreciation for the grandeur of the Italian Alps.

The Italian Alps offer a multitude of outdoor excursions for tourists looking to immerse themselves in nature and discover the region's stunning scenery. Whether strolling along gorgeous routes, carving turns on snowy slopes, or flying high above the mountains, travelers to the Italian Alps are bound to be charmed by its natural beauty and infinite options for adventure and discovery.

- Alpine Cuisine: Culinary Delights of the North

The Alpine areas of northern Italy are not only famed for their breathtaking vistas and outdoor experiences but also for their rich gastronomic traditions. From robust mountain food to delicate alpine delicacies, the cuisine of the Italian Alps reflects the region's distinctive combination of influences and ingredients. Here's a thorough introduction to Alpine cuisine, covering the gastronomic delicacies of the north of Italy:

1. **Local Foods and Flavors**:
- Alpine cuisine is defined by its use of fresh, locally sourced foods that reflect the region's different landscapes and seasonal abundance. From wild herbs and mushrooms to mountain cheeses and cured meats, the tastes of the Alps are as diverse as the region itself.
- Traditional Alpine recipes generally incorporate items such as polenta, potatoes, game meats, and dairy products, which are mainstays of the Alpine cuisine. These rich and fulfilling components give fuel and sustenance for inhabitants and tourists alike, particularly during the chilly winter months.

2. **Cheeses**:

- Cheese plays a significant part in Alpine cuisine, with the area producing a broad range of artisanal cheeses that are acclaimed for their quality and taste. Some of the most renowned Alpine cheeses are Fontina from the Aosta Valley, Bitto from Lombardy, and Asiago from Veneto.

- These cheeses are typically used in classic meals like fondue, raclette, and tartiflette, where they are melted and served with bread, potatoes, or cured meats. Cheese also featured strongly in recipes like gnocchi alla Bava, a creamy potato dumpling dish topped with melted cheese and butter.

3. **Charcuterie and Cured Meats**:

- Cured meats are another feature of Alpine cuisine, with the area producing a range of tasty sausages, salamis, and hams. These meats are commonly seasoned with local herbs and spices, then air-dried or smoked to retain their taste and texture.

- Some of the most popular Alpine charcuterie are bresaola from Lombardy, speck from South Tyrol, and lardo from Alto Adige. These meats are often served thinly sliced as part of an antipasto plate or integrated into meals like pasta, risotto, and soups.

4. **Polenta**:

- Polenta is a cornerstone of Alpine cuisine, functioning as a versatile and soothing staple that is eaten in several ways. Made from finely crushed cornmeal, polenta may be served soft and creamy, or let to set and then grilled, fried, or baked until golden and crisp.

- Polenta is commonly served as an addition to robust meat stews, braised meals, and game meats, offering a delicious basis for soaking up aromatic sauces and gravies. It may also be served as a solitary dish, topped with cheese, mushrooms, or roasted veggies for a simple but tasty supper.

5. **Game Meats**:

- The Alpine mountains of northern Italy are home to a vast range of game species, including deer, wild boar, and hare, which are hunted responsibly and utilized in traditional Alpine recipes. Game meats are regarded for their rich taste and lean texture, making them a preferred option for robust stews, roasts, and braises.

- Venison stew, wild boar ragu, and roasted hare are just a few examples of the robust animal dishes that are eaten across the Alps. These foods are generally seasoned with fragrant herbs and spices and then slow-cooked until soft and tasty.

6. **Alpine Herbs and Wild Foods**:

- Alpine cuisine makes use of a range of wild herbs, berries, and mushrooms that are foraged from the mountains and woods. These ingredients give depth and complexity to recipes, imbuing them with the particular tastes of the alpine landscape.

- Wild mushrooms like porcini, chanterelles, and morels are praised for their earthy taste and meaty texture and are typically used in risottos, pasta dishes, and sauces. Alpine herbs such as thyme, sage, and juniper are used to season meats, soups, and stews, providing a fragrant and aromatic touch to the food.

7. **Desserts and Pastries**:

- No supper in the Alps would be complete without a sweet treat to end it off. Alpine sweets and pastries generally contain seasonal fruits, nuts, and dairy products, exhibiting the region's wealth in a range of tasty and luxurious creations.

- Apple strudel, linzer torte, and sacher torte are just a few examples of the iconic sweets that are loved across the Alps. These desserts are commonly served with a dab of whipped cream or a scoop of vanilla ice cream, adding a touch of richness and luxury to the meal.

Alpine cuisine is a reflection of the region's rough terrain, rich cultural past, and seasonal abundance. From substantial mountain food to delicate alpine delicacies, the culinary traditions of the Italian Alps provide a tempting diversity of tastes and textures to excite the senses and satisfy the appetite. Whether relishing a bowl of creamy polenta, indulging in a piece of pungent cheese or experiencing a sweet and aromatic dessert, travelers visiting the Alps are likely to be charmed by the exquisite treats that await them.

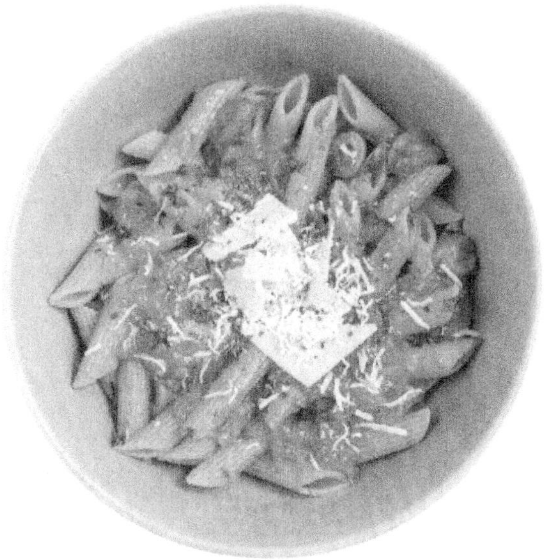

Chapter 3: Venturing Through Central Italy: The Heartland

Central Italy, frequently referred to as the center of the nation, is an area rich in history, culture, and natural beauty. From the rolling hills of Tuscany to the ancient ruins of Rome, Central Italy offers travelers a thrilling trip through centuries of culture and history. Here's a thorough guide on trekking around Central Italy:

- **Introduction to Central Italy**

Central Italy is a region of unparalleled beauty, cultural richness, and historical significance, often referred to as the heart of the country. Encompassing iconic cities such as Rome, Florence, and Siena, as well as charming hill towns, verdant countryside, and breathtaking coastlines, Central Italy offers visitors a captivating journey through centuries of civilization and tradition. Here's an introduction to Central Italy, providing insight into its geography, history, culture, and attractions:

1. **Geography and Landscape**:

- Central Italy is located in the heart of the Italian peninsula, stretching from the northern borders of Tuscany to the southern shores of Lazio and Campania. It is bordered by the Apennine Mountains to the east and the Tyrrhenian Sea to the west, providing a diverse range of landscapes and climates.

- The region is characterized by its rolling hills, fertile valleys, and picturesque coastlines, dotted with vineyards, olive groves, and medieval villages. The Apennine Mountains dominate the eastern portion of Central Italy, offering opportunities for hiking, skiing, and outdoor adventure.

- Along the coast, the Tyrrhenian Sea provides stunning views of rugged cliffs, sandy beaches, and crystal-clear waters. The Amalfi Coast, the Cinque Terre, and the Tuscan Archipelago are just a few of the coastal gems that draw visitors from around the world with their beauty and charm.

2. **Historical Significance**:
   - Central Italy is steeped in history, with a legacy that spans thousands of years. The region was home to the ancient Etruscans, who established a thriving civilization in the area long before the rise of Rome. Etruscan ruins, such as those in Tarquinia and Volterra, offer a glimpse into this ancient culture.
   - Rome, the capital of Italy and one of the world's most historic cities, was the center of the Roman Empire and remains a testament to its grandeur and power. Landmarks such as the Colosseum, the Roman Forum, and the Pantheon attract millions of visitors each year, while the Vatican City, with its iconic St. Peter's Basilica and the Sistine Chapel, is a pilgrimage site for Catholics and a UNESCO World Heritage Site.
   - Florence, the birthplace of the Renaissance, was the epicenter of art, literature, and philosophy in the 14th and 15th centuries. Masterpieces by artists such as Michelangelo, Leonardo da Vinci, and Botticelli adorn the city's churches,

museums, and palaces, while landmarks such as the Duomo, the Uffizi Gallery, and the Ponte Vecchio are testaments to its cultural significance.

3. **Cultural Heritage**:

- Central Italy is a treasure trove of art, architecture, and cultural heritage, with each city and town boasting its own unique traditions and attractions. Siena, with its medieval cityscape and annual Palio horse race, offers a glimpse into Italy's medieval past, while Assisi, the birthplace of St. Francis, is a pilgrimage site for Catholics and a UNESCO World Heritage Site.

- Tuscan cuisine is celebrated for its simple yet flavorful dishes, such as ribollita (a hearty vegetable soup), pappa al pomodoro (bread and tomato soup), and bistecca alla fiorentina (Florentine steak). Umbrian cuisine, on the other hand, is known for its use of wild mushrooms, truffles, and olive oil, while the coastal regions of Lazio and Campania are renowned for their fresh seafood and pasta dishes.

- Central Italy is also known for its wine production, with regions like Tuscany, Umbria, and Lazio producing some of Italy's most iconic wines. Sangiovese, Montepulciano, and Sagrantino are just a few of the grape varietals grown in the region, yielding red wines that are prized for their depth, complexity, and aging potential.

4. **Natural Beauty**:

- In addition to its rich cultural heritage, Central Italy is blessed with stunning natural beauty, with landscapes that range from verdant valleys and rolling hills to rugged mountains and picturesque coastlines. The Tuscan countryside, with its iconic cypress trees and vine-clad hills, is a UNESCO World Heritage Site and a favorite destination for wine lovers and nature enthusiasts.

- The Umbrian countryside, known as the "green heart of Italy," is characterized by its lush forests, pristine rivers, and picturesque hilltop towns. The region's national parks, including the Parco Nazionale dei Monti Sibillini and the Parco Regionale del Monte

Subasio, offer opportunities for hiking, birdwatching, and outdoor recreation.

- Along the coast, the Amalfi Coast and the Cinque Terre are renowned for their stunning scenery, rugged cliffs, and colorful fishing villages. Visitors can explore the coastal trails, swim in the crystal-clear waters, or relax on the sun-drenched beaches, soaking in the beauty of the Mediterranean landscape.

Central Italy is a region of unparalleled beauty, cultural richness, and historical significance, offering visitors a captivating journey through the heart of the country. Whether exploring ancient ruins, savoring regional cuisine, or soaking in the natural beauty of the countryside, travelers to Central Italy are sure to be enchanted by its timeless charm and timeless allure.

- **Tuscany: Rolling Hills and Renaissance Cities**

Tuscany, situated in central Italy, is a region famed for its magnificent scenery, rich cultural history, and creative legacy. From the distinctive rolling hills of the countryside to the majestic Renaissance towns of Florence, Siena, and Pisa, Tuscany offers tourists a mesmerizing combination of natural beauty, history, and creativity. Here's a full tour of Tuscany:

1. **Geography and Landscape**:
- Tuscany is defined by its diversified topography, which contains rolling hills, rich valleys, and jagged coastline. The area is located in central Italy, bounded by the Apennine Mountains to the east and the Tyrrhenian Sea to the west, giving a wonderful background for exploration.
- The undulating hills of Tuscany, commonly represented in Renaissance art, are covered with vineyards, olive groves, and cypress trees, producing a gorgeous scene that has come to characterize the area. The Val d'Orcia and the Chianti Classico area are especially recognized for their scenic beauty and agricultural wealth.
- Along the coast, the Tuscan Riviera provides sandy beaches, crystal-clear waters,

and attractive coastal villages such as Viareggio, Forte dei Marmi, and Castiglione della Pescaia. The Maremma area, with its wild and untouched shoreline, is a paradise for nature lovers and outdoor enthusiasts.

2. **Historical Significance**:
- Tuscany possesses a rich historical legacy that extends back to the Etruscans, who occupied the area before the birth of Rome. The Etruscans left behind a legacy of massive tombs, temples, and artifacts, which may still be seen at archaeological sites such as Volterra, Chiusi, and Tarquinia.
- The Renaissance thrived in Tuscany, with towns like Florence, Siena, and Pisa becoming centers of art, architecture, and culture in the 14th and 15th centuries. Florence, in particular, was the cradle of the Renaissance and is home to masterpieces by painters such as Michelangelo, Leonardo da Vinci, and Botticelli.
- Tuscany is also famed for its ancient hill towns, such as San Gimignano, Volterra, and Montepulciano, which are famous for their well-preserved architecture, narrow

cobblestone alleys, and panoramic views of the surrounding countryside.

3. Cultural Legacy:

- Tuscany is a treasure mine of art, architecture, and cultural legacy, with each city and village having its own distinct traditions and attractions. Florence, the capital of Tuscany, is home to world-renowned museums such as the Uffizi Gallery, the Accademia Gallery, and the Bargello, which hold treasures of Renaissance art and sculpture.

- Siena, with its historic skyline and annual Palio horse race, gives a look into Italy's medieval past, while Pisa is recognized for its distinctive Leaning Tower and Piazza dei Miracoli, a UNESCO World Heritage Site. Lucca, with its well-preserved Renaissance walls and medieval center, is another treasure of Tuscan architecture and culture.

- Tuscan cuisine is recognized for its simplicity, freshness, and quality ingredients, with dishes such as ribollita (a hearty vegetable soup), pappa al pomodoro (bread and tomato soup), and bistecca alla

Fiorentina (Florentine steak) displaying the region's culinary legacy. The Chianti Classico wine area, noted for its Sangiovese grapes and world-class wines, is a favored visit for wine enthusiasts and foodies alike.

4. **Natural Beauty**:
- In addition to its cultural legacy, Tuscany is endowed with magnificent natural beauty, with landscapes that vary from rolling hills and lush valleys to craggy mountains and attractive shorelines. The Val d'Orcia, with its gently undulating hills and charming towns, is a UNESCO World Heritage Site and a favored location for photographers and artists.
- The Chianti Classico area, with its vine-clad hills and historic castles, provides picturesque drives and wine-tasting trips that display the region's agricultural riches and cultural legacy. The Maremma area, with its wild and pristine landscapes, is a haven for nature lovers and outdoor enthusiasts, giving chances for hiking, cycling, and animal viewing.

5. **Artisanal Crafts and Traditions**:

- Tuscany is famed for its artisanal crafts and traditional industries, which have been handed down through centuries. The area is recognized for its pottery, leather items, and textiles, with cities like Montelupo Fiorentino, San Miniato, and Prato noted for their craftsmanship and creative traditions.
- The town of Carrara, situated in the Apuan Alps, is famed for its marble quarries, which have provided marble for some of the world's most iconic statues and monuments, including Michelangelo's David and the Duomo in Florence. Visitors may enjoy guided tours of the quarries and observe firsthand the skill that goes into removing and crafting the marble.

Tuscany is an area of incomparable beauty, cultural richness, and historical importance, providing travelers a compelling trip into the heart of Italy. Whether discovering the Renaissance masterpieces of Florence, relishing the delicacies of Tuscan food, or soaking in the natural beauty of the countryside, tourists visiting Tuscany are likely to be fascinated by its ageless charm and timeless attraction.

- **Emilia-Romagna: Gastronomic Capital and Historic Towns**

Emilia-Romagna, situated in northern Italy, is a region recognized for its rich gastronomic legacy, medieval cities, and cultural treasures. From the historic city of Bologna to the coastal towns of Rimini and Riccione, Emilia-Romagna offers tourists a mesmerizing combination of gourmet pleasures, cultural riches, and natural beauty. Here's a full overview of Emilia-Romagna:

1. **Geography and Landscape**:
- Emilia-Romagna is located in northern Italy, flanked by the Apennine Mountains to the south and the Adriatic Sea to the east. The region's diversified topography contains rolling hills, rich plains, and a lovely coastline, giving a wonderful background for exploration.
- The Po River Valley, which flows through the heart of Emilia-Romagna, is one of

Italy's most productive agricultural areas, noted for its vineyards, orchards, and fields of wheat and maize. The region's rich soil and moderate temperature make it excellent for agriculture, with delicacies like Parmigiano Reggiano cheese, Prosciutto di Parma, and traditional balsamic vinegar of Modena coming from the area.

- Along the Adriatic coast, Emilia-Romagna features some of Italy's most popular beach destinations, including Rimini, Riccione, and Cervia. The beautiful beaches, warm seas, and active nightlife draw millions of tourists each year, making it a favored location for sun-seekers and vacationers.

2. **Historical Significance**:

- Emilia-Romagna is rich in history, with a heritage that dates back to ancient times. The territory was inhabited by the Etruscans and the Celts before being overrun by the Romans, who left behind a rich architectural history that can still be seen in towns like Bologna, Ravenna, and Rimini.

- Bologna, the capital of Emilia-Romagna, is one of Italy's most historic towns, with a wealth of medieval and Renaissance architecture, including the landmark Two Towers and the Basilica of San Petronio. The city's university, established in 1088, is the oldest in the Western world and has played a vital role in establishing Bologna's intellectual and cultural life.

- Ravenna, a UNESCO World Heritage Site, is famed for its beautiful Byzantine mosaics, which cover the city's churches and monuments. The Mausoleum of Galla Placidia, the Basilica of San Vitale, and the Baptistery of Neon are just a few of the architectural gems that make Ravenna a must-visit destination for art and history enthusiasts.

3. **Culinary Heritage**:

- Emilia-Romagna is commonly referred to as the "gastronomic capital" of Italy, with a culinary legacy that is admired across the world. The area is recognized for its fresh, locally sourced foods, traditional recipes, and artisanal culinary items.

- Bologna, in particular, is noted for its rich and hearty food, with dishes such as tagliatelle al ragù (Bolognese sauce), tortellini in brodo (tortellini in broth), and mortadella (Bologna's famous cured meat) coming from the city. Other delicacies of the area include Parmigiano Reggiano cheese, Prosciutto di Parma, and Aceto Balsamico Tradizionale di Modena (traditional balsamic vinegar of Modena).

- Emilia-Romagna is also recognized for its wine production, with districts like the Colli Bolognesi, the Colli Piacentini, and the Romagna hills producing a range of wines, including Sangiovese, Lambrusco, and Albania. Visitors may visit the region's vineyards and wineries, taste the local wines, and learn about the winemaking process from skilled vintners.

4. **Artistic and Cultural Treasures**:

- In addition to its gastronomic pleasures, Emilia-Romagna is home to a wealth of artistic and cultural treasures. The city of Modena, a UNESCO World Heritage Site, includes a beautiful Romanesque church, the Ducal Palace, and the Ghirlandina Tower, which dominate the city's skyline.

- The town of Ferrara, another UNESCO World Heritage Site, is famed for its well-preserved Renaissance architecture, especially the magnificent Castello Estense and the Palazzo dei Diamanti. The city's old core, with its labyrinth of cobblestone lanes and medieval buildings, is a treat to explore on foot.
- Rimini, on the Adriatic coast, is notable for its ancient Roman remains, notably the Arch of Augustus, the Tiberius Bridge, and the Amphitheater of Rimini. The city's active nightlife, beautiful beaches, and dynamic atmosphere make it a popular destination for visitors and residents alike.

5. **Natural Beauty and Outdoor Activities**:
- Emilia-Romagna is endowed with spectacular natural beauty, with landscapes that vary from rolling hills and lush woods to sandy beaches and crystal-clear waterways. The region's national parks, notably the Parco Nazionale delle Foreste Casentinesi, Monte Falterona e Campigna, and the Parco Regionale del Delta del Po,

provide chances for hiking, cycling, and animal watching.

- Along the Adriatic coast, tourists may enjoy a range of water sports and activities, including swimming, sailing, and windsurfing. The Romagna Riviera, with its sandy beaches, mild seas, and vibrant beach resorts, is a favored location for sun-seekers and water sports lovers.

Emilia-Romagna is a region of exceptional beauty, gastronomic quality, and cultural richness, providing travelers a compelling trip into the heart of Italy. Whether visiting ancient cities, relishing traditional food, or soaking in the natural beauty of the countryside, tourists to Emilia-Romagna are likely to be delighted by its timeless charm and dynamic vitality.

- **Marche and Umbria: Hidden Gems of Central Italy**

Marche and Umbria, situated in the heart of central Italy, are two areas that frequently stay unexplored by visitors, although they are rich in natural beauty, cultural legacy, and gastronomic pleasures. From the ancient hilltop villages of Umbria to the beautiful beaches of Marche, these hidden jewels give travelers a treasure trove of experiences waiting to be discovered. Here's a full examination of Marche and Umbria:

1. **Geography and Landscape**:
- Marche and Umbria are located in central Italy, bounded by Tuscany to the west, Emilia-Romagna to the north, and Lazio to the south. The areas are defined by their various scenery, which comprises undulating hills, lush plains, and steep mountains.

- Marche is noted for its magnificent coastline, with sandy beaches, craggy cliffs, and attractive fishing towns dotting the Adriatic coast. The Conero Riviera, with its turquoise waves and white limestone cliffs, is a favored location for beachgoers and nature enthusiasts.

- Umbria, frequently referred to as the "green heart of Italy," is noted for its lush scenery, scenic lakes, and gorgeous valleys. The region's capital, Perugia, is set on a hill overlooking the Tiber Valley and is famed for its medieval architecture, Etruscan fortifications, and thriving cultural life.

2. **Historical and Cultural History**:

- Marche and Umbria possess a rich historical and cultural history, with a legacy that stretches back to ancient times. The cities of Assisi, Spoleto, and Orvieto in Umbria are notable for their well-preserved medieval architecture, ancient cathedrals, and artistic riches.

- Marche is home to the UNESCO World Heritage Site of Urbino, a Renaissance city noted for its beautiful Ducal Palace and old university. Other prominent cities in Marche include Ancona, with its ancient Roman remains and active harbor, and Ascoli Piceno, with its lovely piazzas and Renaissance architecture.

- Both areas are noted for their yearly festivals, religious processions, and cultural events, which highlight local customs, folklore, and food. The Umbria Jazz Festival, held annually in Perugia, is one of the major jazz festivals in Europe and draws performers and music enthusiasts from across the globe.

3. **Culinary Delights**:

- Marche and Umbria are known for their traditional cuisine, which is defined by its simplicity, freshness, and use of locally sourced ingredients. Marche is famed for its seafood dishes, including brodetto (fish stew) and stuffed fried olives, as well as its robust meat dishes, such as porchetta (roast pig) and vincisgrassi (a thick pasta dish).

- Umbrian cuisine, on the other hand, is recognized for its use of wild mushrooms, truffles, and olive oil, as well as its substantial soups, stews, and cured meats. Dishes such as umbrella pasta with black truffles, roasted pigeon, and porchetta are mainstays of the Umbrian diet.

- Both areas are also famed for their wines, with Marche producing crisp and fragrant white wines like Verdicchio and Pecorino, and Umbria producing robust red wines such as Sagrantino and Sangiovese.

4. **Natural Beauty and Outdoor Activities**:

- Marche and Umbria are endowed with spectacular natural beauty, with scenery that varies from rolling hills and vineyards to steep mountains and pure lakes. The Sibillini Mountains, situated on the boundary between Marche and Umbria, provide possibilities for hiking, mountain biking, and animal watching.

- In Umbria, the Monte Subasio Regional Park and the Lake Trasimeno Nature Reserve give options for outdoor leisure, including hiking, birding, and water sports. Marche is home to the Gola del Furlo Nature Reserve, a mountainous canyon formed by the Candigliano River, as well as the Frasassi Caves, a network of subterranean tunnels and stalactite formations.

5. **Artisanal Crafts and Traditions**:

- Marche and Umbria are famed for their artisanal crafts and traditional industries, which have been handed down through centuries. The villages of Fabriano and Urbino in Marche are famed for their papermaking and pottery, while the town of

Norcia in Umbria is known for its cured meats and sausages.

- Both areas are also noted for their festivals and religious processions, which highlight local saints, customs, and folklore. The Corsa dei Ceri, conducted yearly in Gubbio, is one of the oldest and most renowned festivities in Italy, drawing thousands of participants and spectators each year.

Marche and Umbria are hidden treasures of central Italy, providing travelers a richness of natural beauty, cultural legacy, and gastronomic pleasures to uncover. Whether visiting medieval hill villages, relishing traditional food, or soaking in the gorgeous vistas, tourists to Marche and Umbria are bound to be fascinated by the timeless beauty and hidden riches of these lovely areas.

- The Apennines: Nature's Sanctuary and Scenic Drives

The Apennine Mountains, spanning across the length of Italy like a spine, give tourists a refuge of natural beauty, rich wildlife, and beautiful scenery. From rocky peaks and deep valleys to rolling hills and old woods, the Apennines offer a paradise for adventure enthusiasts, nature lovers, and seekers of picturesque drives. Here's a full examination of the Apennines:

1. **Geography and Landscape**:
- The Apennine Mountains, also known as the Appennini in Italian, are the backbone of Italy, stretching about 1,200 kilometers (750 miles) from the northwest to the southeast of the nation. They span from the Ligurian Sea in the northwest to the Adriatic Sea in the southeast, separating the Italian peninsula into two different regions.
- The scenery of the Apennines is vast and varied, marked by rocky peaks, deep valleys, and undulating hills. The highest mountain in the range is Corno Grande, situated in the Gran Sasso massif of the central Apennines, reaching a height of 2,912 meters (9,554 feet) above sea level.
- The Apennines are home to various national parks and natural reserves,

including the Gran Sasso and Monti della Laga National Park, the Maiella National Park, and the Tuscan-Emilian Apennine National Park. These protected regions host a vast variety of flora and wildlife, including uncommon species like the Apennine wolf, the Marsican brown bear, and the Abruzzo chamois.

2. **Outdoor Activities and Recreation**:
- The Apennines provide a multitude of outdoor sports and leisure options for tourists to enjoy. Hiking routes traverse the slopes, allowing access to secluded valleys, alpine meadows, and panoramic overlooks. Popular hiking sites include the Path of the Gods (Sentiero degli Dei) along the Amalfi Coast, the Alta Via dei Monti Liguri in Liguria, and the Apuan Alps in Tuscany.
- The Apennines are also a paradise for cyclists and mountain bikers, with breathtaking routes snaking through stunning scenery, ancient communities, and demanding mountain passes. The Giro d'Italia, one of cycling's Grand Tours, regularly includes stages in the Apennines,

displaying the region's beauty and tough terrain.

- In the winter months, the Apennines change into a paradise for winter sports aficionados, with ski resorts dotting the mountainsides and providing a variety of activities like downhill skiing, cross-country skiing, snowboarding, and snowshoeing.

3. **Scenic Drives and Panoramic Views**:
- One of the greatest ways to appreciate the splendor of the Apennines is by going on a scenic drive via winding mountain roads, panoramic passes, and stunning valleys. The Apennine Strada Statale 63, popularly known as the "SS63," spans the spine of the Apennines, affording stunning views of the surrounding landscape.

- The Strada Statale 42, commonly known as the "SS42" or the "Road of the Apennines Hermitages," weaves its way through the Tuscan-Emilian Apennines, passing past historic hermitages, medieval castles, and attractive hill villages. The road provides spectacular panoramas of the surrounding mountains and valleys, making it a preferred route for scenic drives.

- The Strada Statale 2, often known as the "SS2" or the "Via Cassia," follows the old Roman route that linked Rome to Florence, going through the Apennines and giving vistas of Roman remains, medieval communities, and green scenery along the way.

4. **Cultural and Historical Heritage**:

- The Apennines are rich in history and culture, with a heritage that spans millennia. The mountains are filled with ancient ruins, medieval castles, and historic towns, affording a look into Italy's rich legacy and past.

- The Apennines have been populated from ancient times, with evidence of Neanderthal and Paleolithic villages discovered in caves and rock shelters across the highlands. The area was subsequently occupied by the Etruscans, the Romans, and several medieval civilizations, each leaving their stamp on the scenery and culture of the Apennines.

- The Apennines are also home to a rich heritage of folklore, tales, and religious festivals, which commemorate the natural beauty and spiritual importance of the mountains. Villages like Assisi, Norcia, and San Marino are famed for their yearly festivals, processions, and rituals, which draw tourists from far and wide.

The Apennine Mountains are a nature lover's heaven, providing a refuge of natural beauty, outdoor leisure, and picturesque drives in the heart of Italy. Whether trekking through secluded valleys, skiing down snow-covered slopes, or going on a picturesque drive along winding mountain roads, visitors to the Apennines are likely to be charmed by the spectacular scenery and timeless beauty of this majestic mountain range.

Chapter 4: Exploring Southern Italy: From Coastlines to Countrysides

The southern region of Italy, which is famous for its breathtaking coasts, historic ruins, and scenic countryside, provides tourists with an experience that is both varied and intriguing. It's an aspect of Italy that is rich in history, culture, and breathtaking natural landscapes. From the turquoise seas of the Amalfi Coast to the rugged mountains of Puglia, Southern Italy is a location that does not disappoint. The following is an exhaustive examination of numerous encounters & attractions that are waiting for tourists in Southern Italy:

- Discovering the Charms of Southern Italy

The southern area of Italy is a place that draws tourists to discover its different landscapes and lovely villages. This region is known for its rich tapestry of history, culture, and natural beauty. Southern Italy provides a thrilling trip through centuries of culture and history, from the sun-drenched coasts of Sicily to the ancient remains of Pompeii. This region is home to a wide variety of breathtaking destinations. The following is an exhaustive examination of the allure that Southern Italy has to offer tourists:

1. **Geography and Landscape**:
- Southern Italy is distinguished by its varied topography, which includes rocky beaches, rich plains, and scenery that is both charming and picturesque. As a result of the region's proximity to the Adriatic Sea to the east, the Ionian Sea to the south, and the Tyrrhenian Sea to the west, it is home to a plethora of beaches and coastal landscapes.

-! The Amalfi Coast, a UNESCO World Heritage Site, is one of the most famous places in Southern Italy, with its spectacular cliffs, pastel-colored towns, and panoramic vistas of the Mediterranean Sea. The coastline is lined with lovely villages such as Positano, Amalfi, and Ravello, each giving its own particular appeal and attraction.

-! Inland Southern Italy features undulating hills, olive orchards, and vineyards, as well as steep mountains and national parks. The region's lush soil and Mediterranean temperature make it perfect for agriculture, with crops such as tomatoes, olives, grapes, and citrus fruits growing in the warm sun and rich soil.

2. **Historical and Cultural Heritage**:

- Southern Italy is rich in history, with a past that spans millennia. The area was home to various historical civilizations, including the Greeks, Romans, Byzantines, and Normans, who left behind a plethora of archeological sites, monuments, and ruins.

-! Pompeii and Herculaneum, situated near Naples in the area of Campania, are two of the most renowned archeological sites in Southern Italy, affording tourists a peek into life in ancient Rome. The remains of these ancient settlements, preserved by the eruption of Mount Vesuvius in 79 AD, give a fascinating view into the past.

-! Sicily, the biggest island in the Mediterranean, features a rich cultural legacy that reflects its unique history of Greek, Roman, Arab, Norman, and Spanish influences. The island is home to many UNESCO World Heritage Sites, including the Valley of the Temples in Agrigento, the old core of Syracuse, and the Arab-Norman architecture of Palermo.

3. **Culinary Delights**:

- Southern Italy is famous for its wonderful and varied food, which shows the region's wealth of fresh, locally produced ingredients and traditional recipes.

- Campania is famed for its Neapolitan pizza, produced with San Marzano tomatoes, buffalo mozzarella, and fresh basil, as well as its seafood specialties such as spaghetti alle vongole (spaghetti with clams) and Insalata di mare (seafood salad).

- Puglia, frequently referred to as the "breadbasket of Italy," is noted for its rustic and hearty food, which includes dishes such as orecchiette with broccoli rabe, burrata cheese, and frisella (hard bread) topped with tomatoes and olive oil.

-! Sicilian cuisine is a combination of tastes and influences from throughout the Mediterranean, with dishes such as arancini (rice balls), caponata (eggplant stew), and cannoli (ricotta-filled pastries) delighting the taste buds with their robust flavors and brilliant colors.

4. **Natural Beauty and Outdoor Activities**: - Southern Italy provides a variety of natural beauty and outdoor activities for tourists to enjoy, from hiking and cycling in the countryside to swimming and snorkeling along the shore.

-! The Cilento and Vallo di Diano National Park, situated in the province of Campania, is a UNESCO World Heritage Site and one of the biggest national parks in Italy. The park is home to varied habitats, including mountains, woods, rivers, and shorelines, and provides chances for hiking, animal observation, and outdoor leisure.

-! The Gargano Peninsula, situated in the area of Puglia, is famed for its stunning coastline, white sandy beaches, and crystal-clear seas. Visitors may explore the Gargano National Park, trek along the coastal paths, or relax on the sun-drenched beaches of Vieste, Peschici, and Mattinata. Southern Italy is an area of incomparable beauty, history, and culture, providing travelers a broad assortment of sites and experiences to discover. Whether enjoying the breathtaking coastal beauty of the Amalfi Coast, discovering the ancient remains of Pompeii, or relishing the delicacies of Sicilian cuisine, tourists to Southern Italy are likely to be fascinated by the region's ageless appeal and fascinating allure.

- Campania: Naples, Pompeii, and the Amalfi Coast

Campania, situated in southern Italy, is a region rich in history, culture, and natural beauty. From the busy districts of Naples to the ancient ruins of Pompeii and the gorgeous Amalfi Coast, Campania offers travelers a broad assortment of sites and experiences to discover. Here's a full study of the highlights of Campania:

1. **Naples: A City of Contrasts**:
- Naples, the capital city of Campania, is a lively metropolis famed for its rich history, cultural legacy, and gastronomic pleasures. The city's old center, a UNESCO World Heritage Site, is a maze of small streets, colorful buildings, and busy piazzas, where ancient churches, Renaissance palaces, and Baroque architecture merge harmoniously with contemporary life. – Naples is home to a plethora of cultural treasures, including the National Archaeological Museum, which holds one of the best collections of Greek and Roman antiquities in the world, and the Capodimonte Museum, with its remarkable collection of Renaissance and Baroque art.

- The city is also famed for its gastronomy, with dishes like pizza, spaghetti alle vongole (spaghetti with clams), and sfogliatella (a sweet pastry filled with ricotta cheese) impressing guests with its robust tastes and traditional recipes.

2. **Pompeii**: A Window into Ancient Rome:
- Just a short drive from Naples is the ancient city of Pompeii, a UNESCO World Heritage Site and one of the most significant archeological sites in the world. Pompeii was buried by the explosion of Mount Vesuvius in 79 AD, preserving its streets, houses, and artifacts in remarkable detail.
- Visitors to Pompeii may visit the remains of temples, villas, and bathhouses, as well as the world-famous plaster casts of the victims of the eruption. The site gives a unique peek into everyday life in ancient Rome, with paintings, mosaics, and relics offering insights into the culture, economics, and society of the period.

3. **The Amalfi Coast**: A Slice of Paradise:
- The Amalfi Coast, spanning along the southern border of the Sorrentine Peninsula, is one of the most magnificent coasts in the world, with its spectacular cliffs, quaint towns, and turquoise seas. Designated as a UNESCO World Heritage Site, the Amalfi Coast is known for its natural beauty,

medieval villages, and breathtaking landscapes.

- The villages of Amalfi, Positano, and Ravello are among the highlights of the Amalfi Coast, each providing its own particular beauty and attractions. Visitors may meander along cobblestone alleys, observe pastel-colored buildings clinging to the cliffs, and take up the breathtaking views of the Mediterranean Sea.

- The Amalfi Coast is also a heaven for outdoor lovers, with options for trekking along gorgeous routes, bathing in isolated coves, and discovering secret beaches and grottoes. Boat trips and cruises give a unique view of the coastline, enabling guests to find hidden jewels and secret areas unreachable by land.

Campania is an area of contrasts and paradoxes, where ancient history meets contemporary life, and urban sophistication coexists with natural beauty. Whether exploring the busy streets of Naples, finding the mysteries of Pompeii, or soaking up the sun on the Amalfi Coast, tourists visiting

Campania are likely to be enchanted by its ageless appeal and fascinating allure.

- Calabria: The Toe of Italy's Boot

Calabria, located in the southernmost corner of Italy, is an area of rugged beauty, rich history, and lively culture. Known as the "toe" of Italy's boot, Calabria features gorgeous beaches, attractive towns, and historic ruins, making it a tempting location for tourists seeking both rest and adventure. Here's a full overview of Calabria's highlights:

1. **Geography and Landscape**:
- Calabria is flanked by the Ionian Sea to the east and the Tyrrhenian Sea to the west, affording tourists a multitude of coastline landscapes and beaches. The area is known for its rough coastline, with cliffs, coves, and sandy beaches lapped by crystal-clear seas.

-! Inland, Calabria is characterized by mountain ranges, especially the steep Aspromonte and Sila massifs, which rise sharply from the coastal lowlands. The mountains are covered with deep woods, sprinkled with attractive towns, and crisscrossed by hiking paths, affording chances for outdoor exploration and adventure.

2. **Historical and Cultural Legacy**:

- Calabria has a rich history that extends back to ancient times, with influences from Greek, Roman, Byzantine, and Norman civilizations defining its culture and legacy. The area is home to a multitude of archeological monuments, including the ancient Greek city of Locri Epizephyrii, the Roman remains of Capo Colonna and the medieval fortification of Le Castella.

- The town of Cosenza, known as the "Athens of Calabria," features a historic center rich with churches, palaces, and museums, while the seaside town of Tropea is famed for its gorgeous beaches, ancient ruins, and colorful architecture.

- Calabria is also noted for its traditional festivals, religious processions, and culinary traditions, which commemorate the region's cultural identity and legacy. Visitors may enjoy local food, including delicacies like nduja (hot sausage), swordfish, and Calabrian chili peppers, as well as handmade pasta, cheeses, and wines.

3. **Natural Beauty and Outdoor Activities**:

- Calabria's natural beauty is one of its most outstanding qualities, with gorgeous beaches, craggy mountains, and lush woods ready to be discovered. The area is home to many national parks and natural reserves, including the Aspromonte National Park and the Sila National Park, which provide chances for hiking, animal viewing, and outdoor recreation.
- The coastline of Calabria is lined with picturesque beach towns and villages, including Tropea, Pizzo, and Scilla, each having its own particular beauty and attractions. Visitors may swim in the crystal-clear seas, relax on sandy beaches, and discover secret coves and grottoes along the coast.
- Adventure seekers may enjoy sports like snorkeling, scuba diving, sailing, and windsurfing, while nature enthusiasts can explore the region's unique ecosystems, including coastal wetlands, mountain forests, and alpine meadows.

Calabria is an area of remarkable beauty, rich history, and active culture, providing tourists a broad selection of sites and experiences to explore. Whether visiting ancient ruins, soaking up the sun on exquisite beaches, or climbing through steep mountains, tourists to Calabria are likely to be enchanted by its timeless appeal and natural magnificence.

Tropea is a small town on the east coast of Calabria, in southern Italy. It's known for its clifftop historical center, beaches and prized red onions.

- **Puglia: The Heel of Italy's Boot**

Puglia, frequently referred to as the heel of Italy's boot, is a region noted for its gorgeous landscapes, rich history, and unique cultural legacy. From its whitewashed hilltop villages to its magnificent coastline and old olive fields, Puglia offers tourists a compelling combination of history and modernity. Here's a full overview of Puglia's highlights:

1. **Geography and Landscape**:
- Puglia is situated in the southeastern section of Italy, bounded by the Adriatic Sea to the east and the Ionian Sea to the west. Its diversified scenery contains undulating hills, lush plains, and a jagged coastline filled with sandy beaches, rocky coves, and limestone cliffs.
- The area is famed for its olive orchards, which produce some of the best olive oil in Italy. Puglia is home to around 60 million olive trees, many of which are centuries old and constitute a vital part of the region's cultural and agricultural heritage.

- Inland, Puglia is noted by its historic "trulli" cottages, unusual limestone buildings with conical roofs that dot the terrain. The village of Alberobello, a UNESCO World Heritage Site, is noted for its scenic trulli area, where tourists may explore small alleyways dotted with quaint houses.

2. **Historical and Cultural Heritage**:
- Puglia offers a rich history that extends back to ancient times, with influences from Greek, Roman, Byzantine, and Norman cultures forming its cultural legacy. The area is home to various archeological monuments, including the ancient city of Egnazia, the Roman remains of Bari, and the medieval castles of Castel del Monte and Trani.

- The city of Lecce, known as the "Florence of the South," is famed for its Baroque architecture, with exquisite churches, palaces, and piazzas gracing its old center. Lecce's beautiful stone carvings and magnificent façade are a tribute to the region's creative and architectural brilliance.

-! Puglia is also noted for its traditional festivals, religious processions, and culinary traditions, which commemorate the region's cultural identity and legacy. Visitors may taste local food, including meals such as orecchiette pasta with broccoli rabe, grilled octopus, and "taralli" biscuits, as well as locally made wines such as Primitivo and Negroamaro.

3. **Natural Beauty and Outdoor Activities**:
- Puglia's natural beauty is one of its most enticing aspects, with beautiful beaches, coastal marshes, and rolling countryside ready to be discovered. The area is home to various national parks and natural reserves, including the Gargano National Park and the Salento Regional Park, which provide possibilities for hiking, birding, and outdoor recreation.

- The coastline of Puglia is littered with picturesque beach towns and villages, such as Polignano a Mare, Ostuni, and Gallipoli, each having its own particular beauty and attractions. Visitors may swim in the crystal-clear seas, relax on sandy beaches, and discover secret coves and caves along the coast.

- Adventure seekers may enjoy sports like snorkeling, scuba diving, sailing, and windsurfing, while nature enthusiasts can explore the region's unique ecosystems, including coastal dunes, limestone cliffs, and ancient woods.

Puglia is a region of exceptional beauty, rich history, and unique culture, providing tourists a broad assortment of sites and experiences to explore. Whether visiting ancient sites, tasting traditional food, or lounging on beautiful beaches, tourists to Puglia are bound to be fascinated by its timeless appeal and natural magnificence.

- **Sicily: A Mediterranean Jewel**

Sicily, the biggest island in the Mediterranean Sea, is a country of contrasts and complexity, where ancient history, various cultures, and breathtaking scenery mix to create a genuinely compelling destination. From its rich ancient sites to its dynamic towns, stunning coasts, and lush valleys, Sicily gives travelers a multitude of experiences to explore. Here's a full overview of Sicily's highlights:

1. **Geography and Landscape**:
- Sicily is situated at the crossroads of the Mediterranean, strategically positioned between Europe and Africa. Its diversified terrain is distinguished by jagged mountains, rich plains, and a spectacular coastline, with sandy beaches, craggy cliffs, and secret coves dotting its shores.
- The island is dominated by Mount Etna, one of the most active volcanoes in the world and a UNESCO World Heritage Site. Etna's overwhelming presence dominates the landscape of eastern Sicily, with its lush slopes covered with vineyards, orchards, and woods.
-! Inland, Sicily is filled with gorgeous hilltop towns and villages, such as Taormina, Cefalù, and Ragusa, each giving its own particular charm and attractions. The

island's rich valleys, known as "le contrade," are home to citrus groves, olive orchards, and vineyards, producing some of Italy's best fruits, oils, and wines.

2. **Historical and Cultural Heritage**:
- Sicily has a rich and diversified history that spans over 3,000 years, with influences from Greek, Roman, Arab, Norman, and Spanish civilizations creating its cultural legacy. The island is home to various ancient monuments, including the Valley of the Temples near Agrigento, the Greek theater of Syracuse, and the Roman palace of Casale in Piazza Armerina.

- The city of Palermo, the capital of Sicily, is a melting pot of civilizations, with its historic core exhibiting a combination of architectural styles, including Arab, Norman, Gothic, and Baroque. The city's marketplaces, including the bustling Ballarò and Vucciria markets, provide a sensory explosion of sights, sounds, and scents, with merchants offering fresh vegetables, seafood, spices, and local specialties.

- Sicily is also noted for its traditional festivals, religious processions, and culinary traditions, which commemorate the island's cultural identity and legacy. Visitors may taste local food, including delicacies such as arancini (rice balls), pasta alla Norma, and cannoli (ricotta-filled pastries), as well as locally produced wines such as Nero d'Avola and Marsala.

3. **Natural Beauty and Outdoor Activities**:
- Sicily's natural beauty is one of its most enticing qualities, with beautiful beaches, crystal-clear seas, and stunning landscapes begging to be explored. The island is bordered by the Mediterranean Sea, allowing chances for swimming, snorkeling, scuba diving, and sailing.
- The Aeolian Islands, a UNESCO World Heritage Site situated off the northern coast of Sicily, are famed for their volcanic scenery, notably the smoking crater of Stromboli and the boiling mud springs of Vulcano. Visitors may explore the islands by boat, trek along gorgeous paths, and rest on isolated beaches.

- Inland, Sicily's national parks and natural reserves provide chances for trekking, birding, and animal viewing. The Madonie and Nebrodi mountain ranges are home to different ecosystems, including forests, meadows, and alpine lakes, while the Zingaro Nature Reserve and Vendicari Nature Reserve safeguard coastal habitats and marine life.

Sicily is a Mediterranean treasure, with its rich history, diversified culture, and magnificent scenery enticing travelers from across the globe. Whether visiting ancient sites, enjoying local food, or soaking up the sun on beautiful beaches, tourists to Sicily are likely to be fascinated by its timeless charm and natural beauty.

- Sardinia: Island Paradise in the Tyrrhenian Sea

Sardinia, the second-largest island in the Mediterranean Sea, is a treasure mine of natural beauties, ancient history, and distinct culture. Nestled amid the Tyrrhenian Sea, Sardinia captivates travelers with its gorgeous beaches, rocky terrain, and interesting ancient monuments. Here's a full overview of Sardinia's highlights:

1. **Geography and Terrain**:
- Sardinia features a diversified and spectacular terrain, typified by steep mountains, rolling hills, and a gorgeous shoreline. The island is surrounded by crystal-clear seas, with sandy beaches, secret coves, and towering cliffs surrounding its shores.

- The heart of Sardinia is dominated by the Gennargentu mountain range, home to rocky peaks, deep valleys, and lush woods. The highest summit, Punta La Marmora, gives panoramic views of the island and the surrounding sea.

- Sardinia is also noted for its unusual geological formations, notably the limestone cliffs of the Capo Caccia peninsula and the towering granite rock formations of the Gallura area. The island's natural beauty is protected by various national parks and nature reserves, including the Gennargentu National Park and the Asinara National Park.

2. Historical and Cultural Legacy:

- Sardinia has a rich and ancient history that extends back thousands of years, with influences from Phoenician, Carthaginian, Roman, and Byzantine civilizations forming its cultural legacy. The island is home to various archeological monuments, including the ancient nuraghe communities, and megalithic stone constructions peculiar to Sardinia.

- The city of Cagliari, the capital of Sardinia, features a historic core replete with tiny alleyways, ancient cathedrals, and Spanish-influenced architecture. The city's archeological museum, built in a former monastery, shows objects from ancient periods to the Middle Ages.

- Sardinia is also recognized for its traditional festivals, such as the "Cavalcade Sarda" in Sassari and the "Sartiglia" in Oristano, which commemorate the island's cultural identity and legacy. Visitors may sample traditional music, dancing, and food, including delicacies like "proceeds" (roast suckling pig), "culurgiones" (potato-filled pasta), and "pane carasau" (thin, crispy bread).

3. **Natural Beauty and Outdoor Activities**:
- Sardinia's natural beauty is one of its most attractive aspects, with beautiful beaches, crystal-clear oceans, and untouched landscapes begging to be discovered. The island is bordered by some of the greatest diving and snorkeling places in the Mediterranean, with underwater caverns, reefs, and marine life to discover.

- The coastline of Sardinia is speckled with attractive beach towns and villages, such as Alghero, Bosa, and Villasimius, each having its own particular beauty and attractions. Visitors may swim in the turquoise seas, lounge on sandy beaches, and discover secret coves and grottoes along the coast.

- Inland, Sardinia provides chances for hiking, mountain biking, and equestrian riding, with paths snaking through woods, mountains, and valleys. The island's rural sections are peppered with agriturismo farms, where tourists may experience traditional Sardinian living, enjoy local food, and learn about artisanal skills like weaving and ceramics.

Sardinia is an island paradise in the Tyrrhenian Sea, with its breathtaking scenery, rich history, and lively culture enticing travelers from across the globe. Whether visiting ancient ruins, sunbathing on beautiful beaches, or immersing oneself in traditional Sardinian life, tourists to Sardinia are likely to be fascinated by its timeless appeal and natural beauty.

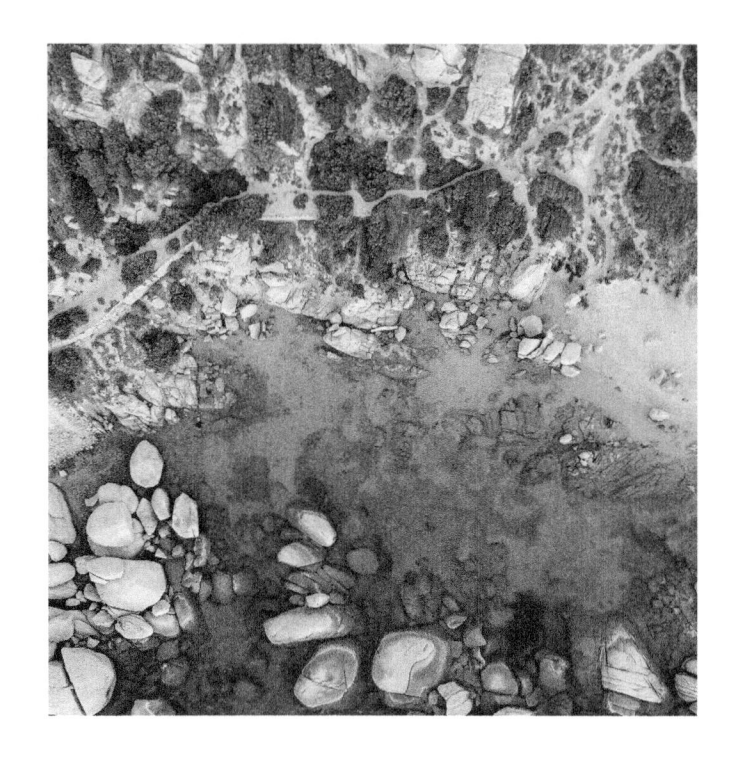

Porto pollo

Church on the edge
Sardinia, Italy

Chapter 5: Immersing Yourself in Italian Culture

Italy, famed for its rich history, diversified landscapes, and dynamic culture, provides tourists a unique chance to immerse themselves in a tapestry of traditions, rituals, and experiences that have molded the country's character for generations. From the busy streets of its ancient cities to the calm countryside and attractive seaside villages, Italy begs tourists to explore its timeless appeal and embrace its cultural heritage. Here's a full discussion of how to immerse oneself in Italian culture:

- Art and Architecture: Masterpieces Across Italy

Italy, frequently referred to as the birthplace of Western civilization, is known for its unrivaled creative history and architectural treasures. From ancient ruins to Renaissance masterpieces and Baroque splendors, the nation possesses a treasure trove of creative treasures that span millennia. Here's a complete overview of some of the most recognizable art and architectural wonders around Italy:

1. **Ancient Rome**:
- The Colosseum: One of Rome's most renowned monuments, the Colosseum is a representation of the majesty and might of ancient Rome. Built in the 1st century AD, this amphitheater could seat up to 80,000 people and held gladiatorial fights, animal hunts, and public performances.
- The Roman Forum: Once the political, religious, and commercial hub of ancient Rome, the Roman Forum is a large archeological site filled with remains of temples, basilicas, and government structures. Highlights include the Temple of Saturn, the Arch of Septimius Severus, and the House of the Vestals.

2. **Florence**:
- The Duomo: Florence's cathedral, Santa Maria del Fiore, is a masterpiece of Gothic architecture, capped by Brunelleschi's distinctive dome. Visitors may ascend to the

top of the dome for panoramic views of the city and appreciate the exquisite marble facade and Giotto's bell tower.

- The Uffizi Gallery: Home to one of the most significant art collections in the world, the Uffizi Gallery holds masterpieces by Renaissance painters such as Botticelli, Michelangelo, Leonardo da Vinci, and Raphael. Highlights include Botticelli's "The Birth of Venus" and Leonardo's "Annunciation."

3. Venice:
- St. Mark's Basilica: This Byzantine masterpiece is one of the most renowned cathedrals in Italy, noted for its stunning mosaics, complex marble flooring, and golden altarpiece. The basilica's golden domes and beautiful exterior are a monument to Venice's richness and influence throughout the Middle Ages.

- The Doge's Palace: Once the palace of the doges of Venice and the center of Venetian government, the Doge's Palace is a masterpiece of Venetian Gothic architecture. Visitors may tour its majestic halls, opulent apartments, and famed Bridge of Sighs, which linked the palace to the jail.

4. **Rome**:

- The Vatican Museums: Home to one of the finest art collections in the world, the Vatican Museums contain works by Michelangelo, Raphael, Caravaggio, and numerous more painters. Highlights include Michelangelo's Sistine Chapel ceiling and Raphael's "School of Athens."

- St. Peter's Basilica: The biggest church in the world, St. Peter's Basilica is a marvel of Renaissance design, with its towering dome, marble exterior, and colossal interior. Visitors may appreciate Michelangelo's Pieta and Bernini's Baldachin, as well as ascend to the top of the dome for panoramic views of Rome.

5. **Pisa**:

- The Leaning Tower of Pisa: One of Italy's most renowned monuments, the Leaning Tower of Pisa is a symbol of the city's architectural brilliance and technical ability. Built as a standalone bell tower for the neighboring cathedral, the tower's tilt started during construction owing to unstable terrain, producing a distinctive and famous landmark.

6. **Naples**:

- The Archaeological Museum: Home to one of the most significant collections of ancient Roman antiquities in the world, the Archaeological Museum in Naples contains treasures from Pompeii, Herculaneum, and other archaeological sites in the vicinity. Highlights include mosaics, frescoes, and sculptures representing scenes of everyday life in ancient Rome.

7. **Milan**:

- The Last Supper: Leonardo da Vinci's masterwork, "The Last Supper," is preserved in the refectory of the Convent of Santa Maria delle Grazie in Milan. This legendary fresco, painted between 1495 and 1498, represents the moment Jesus discloses that one of his followers would betray him and is known for its emotional intensity and technical ingenuity.

Italy's art and architecture are a monument to the country's rich history, cultural richness, and creative brilliance. From the grandeur of ancient Rome to the magnificence of the Renaissance and beyond, Italy's masterpieces continue to inspire and enchant tourists from across the globe, giving a peek into the country's history and its ongoing heritage of creativity and craftsmanship.

- Culinary Traditions: From Pizza to Pasta

Italian food is famous internationally for its simplicity, freshness, and depth of taste. From substantial pasta meals to crispy pizzas and delectable sweets, Italy's culinary traditions reflect the country's rich history, various regions, and seasonal ingredients. Here's a complete overview of some of the most renowned foods and culinary traditions throughout Italy:

1. **Pasta**:
- Pasta is a mainstay of Italian cuisine, with hundreds of forms and types to select from. From long, thin strands of spaghetti to

twisted fusilli and filled ravioli, pasta recipes are adored for their diversity and adaptability.

- Classic pasta meals include spaghetti carbonara, cooked with eggs, cheese, pancetta, and black pepper; fettuccine alfredo, tossed in a creamy sauce of butter and Parmesan cheese; and lasagna, layered with meat sauce, cheese, and bechamel.

-! Each area of Italy has its own trademark pasta recipes, such as orecchiette with broccoli rabe in Puglia, trofie with pesto in Liguria, and pappardelle with wild boar ragu in Tuscany.

2. **Pizza**:

- Pizza is undoubtedly Italy's most renowned culinary export, with its roots reaching back to ancient Rome and Naples. Traditional Neapolitan pizza is composed of basic, high-quality ingredients, like San Marzano tomatoes, mozzarella cheese, and fresh basil, cooked in a wood-fired oven for a crispy, charred crust.

- Classic pizza variants include Margherita, topped with tomato sauce, mozzarella cheese, and basil leaves; marinara, with tomato sauce, garlic, oregano, and olive oil; and quattro stagioni, split into four portions with various toppings reflecting the four seasons.

- Pizza has changed throughout time, with varieties such as Roman-style pizza, which has a thinner crust and is commonly served al taglio (by the slice), and gourmet pizzas topped with uncommon ingredients such as truffles, prosciutto, and arugula.

3. **Antipasti and Appetizers**:
- Italian dinners frequently begin with antipasti, a selection of appetizers that reflect the tastes and ingredients of the area. Antipasti may contain cured meats such as prosciutto and salami, marinated vegetables like artichokes and olives, and cheeses such as mozzarella and pecorino.

- Bruschetta, toasted bread covered with tomatoes, garlic, and olive oil, is a favorite antipasto dish, as are crostini, tiny pieces of bread topped with spreads such as chicken liver pate or ricotta cheese.

- Seafood fans may have fritto misto, a mixed seafood plate of fried shrimp, calamari, and fish, or Insalata di mare, a salad of mixed seafood marinated in lemon juice and olive oil.

4. **Main Meals**:
- Italian main meals frequently include fresh, seasonal ingredients and uncomplicated preparations that allow the natural flavors to show. Seafood meals are popular along the beaches, with specialties such as spaghetti alle vongole (spaghetti with clams), risotto ai frutti di mare (seafood risotto), and pesce al forno (baked fish) with lemon and herbs.

- Meat dishes are particularly prevalent in Italian cuisine, with favorites such as ossobuco, braised veal shanks with vegetables and gremolata; pollo alla cacciatora, chicken cooked with tomatoes, onions, and herbs; and bistecca alla Fiorentina, a grilled T-bone steak seasoned with olive oil and rosemary.

- Vegetarians may enjoy delicacies such as eggplant parmigiana, layers of fried eggplant, tomato sauce, and cheese baked till bubbling; risotto ai funghi, creamy risotto with wild mushrooms; and Caprese salad, prepared with fresh tomatoes, mozzarella cheese, and basil leaves drizzled with olive oil.

5. **Dolci and Desserts**:
- Italian desserts are a delicious ending to every dinner, with a vast array of delicacies to suit every palate. Tiramisu, a creamy dessert created with layers of coffee-soaked ladyfingers and mascarpone cheese, is a traditional delight.
- Cannoli, crispy pastry shells filled with rich ricotta cheese and chocolate chips, are a renowned Sicilian delicacy, while gelato, Italy's version of ice cream, comes in a rainbow of flavors, from basic pistachio and chocolate to unique fruit and nut combinations.
- Other famous sweets include panna cotta, a smooth custard topped with fruit compote or caramel sauce; zabaglione, a frothy delicacy prepared with egg yolks, sugar, and Marsala

wine; and affogato, a simple but delectable treat of vanilla gelato topped with espresso.

6. **Regional Specialties**:

- Each area of Italy has its own distinct culinary traditions and specialties, inspired by local products, cultural history, and historical influences. Here are some prominent regional specialties:

- **Emilia-Romagna**: Known as the culinary center of Italy, Emilia-Romagna is famed for its rich pasta dishes such as tortellini in brodo (meat-filled pasta in broth), tagliatelle al ragù (pasta with meat sauce), and lasagna alla Bolognese. The area is also famed for its cured meats, including prosciutto di Parma and culatello di Zibello, as well as its aged cheeses like Parmigiano-Reggiano and Grana Padano.

- **Tuscany**: Tuscany's rustic cuisine honors simple, fresh ingredients and robust tastes. Ribollita, a substantial soup prepared with bread, vegetables, and beans, is a Tuscan staple, as is pappa al Pomodoro, a thick tomato and bread soup. Florentine steak, grilled T-bone steak seasoned with olive oil and herbs, is another signature dish of the area.

- **Sicily**: Sicilian cuisine is a melting pot of tastes inspired by Greek, Arab, Norman, and Spanish cultures. Arancini, deep-fried rice balls loaded with meat, cheese, or vegetables, are a famous street food snack, while caponata, a sweet and sour eggplant relish, is a beloved antipasto dish. Sicily is also renowned for its sweet delights such as cannoli, cassata, and granita.

- **Campania**: Home to Naples and the Amalfi Coast, Campania is famed for its pizza, pasta, and seafood delicacies. Neapolitan pizza, with its thin crust and basic toppings, is a UNESCO-recognized cultural property. Pasta recipes such as spaghetti alle vongole (spaghetti with clams) and linguine alle cozze (linguine with mussels) reflect the region's bountiful seafood.

- **Piedmont**: Piedmontese cuisine is recognized for its rich, substantial tastes and utilization of local delicacies such as truffles, mushrooms, and hazelnuts.

Agnolotti del plin, little pasta packages stuffed with meat or vegetables, are a regional delicacy, as is bagna cauda, a warm dip prepared with anchovies, garlic, and olive oil, eaten with fresh vegetables.

- **Veneto**: Venetian cuisine is inspired by its marine setting and contains a range of seafood dishes such as risotto al nero di sepia (risotto with cuttlefish ink) and sarde in saor (marinated sardines). Veneto is also famed for its polenta, a creamy cornmeal porridge eaten with a variety of toppings such as mushroom ragù or braised meats.
- **Lombardy**: Lombard cuisine is defined by its use of butter, cheese, and hearty meats. Risotto alla Milanese, a saffron-infused risotto seasoned with bone marrow, is a hallmark dish of Milan, while ossobuco, braised veal shanks served with gremolata, is a regional delicacy. Gorgonzola and Taleggio cheeses are also made in Lombardy.
- **Sardinia**: Sardinian cuisine reflects the island's pastoral heritage and includes dishes such as culurgiones, Sardinian ravioli

stuffed with potato and cheese, and malloreddus, little pasta forms eaten with a tomato and sausage sauce. Sardinia is also noted for its pecorino cheese, manufactured from sheep's milk, and its mirto liquor, created from myrtle berries.

Italian culinary traditions are strongly ingrained in the country's history, geography, and cultural heritage, making each dish a celebration of Italy's many regions and culinary past. Whether relishing a dish of handmade pasta at a family-run trattoria or enjoying a piece of pizza on a crowded piazza, dining in Italy is an experience that thrills the senses and feeds the spirit.

- **Wine and Gastronomy: A Tour of Italian Flavors**

Italy's rich culinary tradition is tightly entwined with its thriving wine culture, making it a haven for food and wine connoisseurs alike. From the sun-drenched vineyards of Tuscany to the scenic hills of

Piedmont and the seaside districts of Sicily, Italy's various landscapes generate a stunning assortment of wines that complement the country's famed cuisine. Here's a full examination of Italian wine and gastronomy:

1. **Wine Regions**:
- Italy is home to 20 different wine regions, each with its own unique terroir, grape varietals, and winemaking traditions. Some of the most notable wine areas include:
- **Tuscany**: Known for its classic Sangiovese-based wines such as Chianti, Brunello di Montalcino, and Vino Nobile di Montepulciano. Tuscany's undulating hills, cypress-lined roads, and old vineyards make it one of Italy's most gorgeous wine regions.
- **Piedmont**: Famous for its fine Nebbiolo grape, which is used to make the famed wines of Barolo and Barbaresco. Piedmont is also noted for its sparkling wine, Asti Spumante, manufactured from the Moscato wine.
- **Veneto**: Home of the famed sparkling wine Prosecco, as well as the beautiful red wines

of Valpolicella and the rich, sweet wines of Amarone della Valpolicella.

- **Sicily**: Italy's biggest island has a broad variety of wines, from the volcanic reds of Mount Etna to the fortified wines of Marsala and the crisp whites of the Etna Bianco.

2. **Grape Types**:
- Italy is home to over 350 indigenous grape types, making it one of the most diversified wine-producing nations in the world. While Sangiovese, Nebbiolo, and Barbera are some of the most regularly planted red grape types, Italy also produces a range of white wines from grapes such as Trebbiano, Vermentino, and Pinot Grigio.

- Each wine area specializes in distinct grape types, typically reflecting the local terroir and climate. For example, the coastal districts of Liguria and Campania are recognized for their crisp, fragrant white wines, while the sun-drenched hills of Sicily create powerful, full-bodied reds.

3. **Wine Styles and Production**:
- Italian wines come in a broad spectrum of types, from light and fruity to strong and

deep. In addition to still wines, Italy is also recognized for its sparkling wines, such as Prosecco, Franciacorta, and Lambrusco, as well as its sweet wines, such as Vin Santo and Moscato d'Asti.

- Winemaking processes differ among areas and producers, with some winemakers clinging to traditional methods handed down through generations, while others embrace contemporary technology and innovation. Many wineries in Italy are family-owned and run, with a profound regard for heritage and a devotion to quality.

4. **Food and Wine Pairing**:

- Italian food is notably varied, with each area presenting its own peculiarities and tastes. Pairing wine with food is a fundamental aspect of the Italian dining experience, with different wines complimenting certain meals and components.

- Light, acidic white wines such as Vermentino and Soave combine nicely with seafood meals, while medium-bodied reds such as Chianti and Barbera are great for pasta with tomato-based sauces or grilled meats. Rich, full-bodied reds such as Barolo and Amarone are best served with heavy foods such as osso buco or aged cheeses.

5. **Wine Tourism**:

- Wine tourism is a burgeoning sector in Italy, with travelers coming to wine areas to experience vineyards, wineries, and tasting rooms. Many vineyards provide guided tours and tastings, enabling visitors to learn about the winemaking process and taste a range of wines.

- In addition to wine tastings, wine visitors may also enjoy culinary activities like cooking workshops, vineyard picnics, and gourmet dinners matched with local wines. Wine festivals and events are hosted throughout the year, highlighting the finest of Italian wine and food.

Italy's wine and food provide a fascinating tour through the country's rich culture, history, and terroir. Whether enjoying a glass of Sangiovese in Tuscany, indulging in a meal of pasta in Piedmont, or eating seafood on the coasts of Sicily, experiencing Italy's culinary pleasures is a feast for the senses that makes a lasting effect on those who participate.

- Festivals and Celebrations: Experiencing Italy's Vibrant Culture

Italy's complex tapestry of festivals and festivities reflects the country's broad cultural past, religious traditions, and love for life. From colorful carnivals and religious processions to gastronomic festivals and historical reenactments, Italy's calendar is full of events that bring communities together and reflect the country's distinctive personality. Here's a complete overview of some of Italy's most lively festivals and celebrations:

1. **Carnevale di Venezia (Venice Carnival)**:
- Held annually in Venice, the Carnival is one of Italy's most renowned and lavish festivities. Dating back to the 12th century, the Carnival is famed for its spectacular masks, costumes, and masquerade balls.

Visitors may meander around the streets of Venice, where performers in magnificent costumes and masks entertain audiences with music, dance, and drama.

2. Il Palio di Siena (Siena Palio):
- The Palio is a traditional horse race conducted twice a year in the ancient city of Siena, in Tuscany. Ten riders from various areas (contrade) fight in an exciting bareback sprint around the Piazza del Campo, Siena's largest plaza. The Palio is preceded by colorful processions, flag-waving celebrations, and traditional feasts.

3. Festa della Repubblica (Republic Day):
- Celebrated on June 2nd, Republic Day celebrates the creation of the Italian Republic in 1946. Festivities include parades, concerts, and cultural activities hosted in cities and towns around Italy. In Rome, the President of the Republic presides over a military parade down Via dei Fori Imperiali, followed by a wreath-laying ceremony at the Altare della Patria.

4. Festa di San Giovanni (Feast of St. John):
- Celebrated on June 24th, the Feast of St. John is a religious feast commemorating the patron saint of Florence. The climax of the celebrations is the traditional Calcio Storico (historic football) match, a harsh and old kind of football played in Renaissance-era costumes in Piazza Santa Croce. The day culminates with fireworks above the Arno River.

5. Infiorata di Noto (Noto Flower Festival):
- Held yearly in the town of Noto, in Sicily, the Infiorata is a gorgeous floral event when complex carpets of flower petals are put out in complicated arrangements down the streets of the town. The event commemorates the beginning of spring and draws tourists from across the globe who come to see the brilliant flower arrangements.

6. Sagra del Redentore (Redentore Festival):

- Celebrated in Venice on the third weekend of July, the Redentore Festival celebrates the end of the plague in the 16th century. The centerpiece of the celebration is a stunning fireworks show over the Venetian Lagoon, followed by boat processions and eating traditional Venetian cuisine such as sarde in saor (marinated sardines) and frittelle (fried pastries).

7. **La Quintana (The Quintana):**
- Held in Ascoli Piceno, in the Marche area, the Quintana is a medieval jousting contest that goes back to the 17th century. Knights on horseback engage in several equestrian activities, including ring jousting and spear throwing, to win the coveted palio (flag). The event is preceded by a spectacular historical procession through the streets of the city.

8. **La Fiera del Tartufo (Truffle Fair):**
- Held annually in Alba, in the Piedmont area, the Truffle Fair commemorates the treasured white truffle, regarded as the "diamond of the kitchen." The event involves truffle hunts, culinary

demonstrations, and samples of truffle-infused delicacies such as risotto, pasta, and cheese. Visitors may also buy fresh truffles and truffle goods from local merchants.

9. **Processione dei Misteri (Procession of the Mysteries):**
- Held in Trapani, Sicily, the parade of the Mysteries is a solemn religious parade that takes place on Good Friday. Participants carry life-size sculptures portraying scenes from the Passion of Christ through the streets of the city, accompanied by sad chanting and prayers. The procession is a tremendous demonstration of faith and commitment.

10. **La Notte Bianca (White Night):**
- White Nights are celebrated in many towns throughout Italy, including Rome, Florence, and Naples, when shops, restaurants, and cultural institutions remain open late into the night, presenting special events, concerts, and plays. The streets come alive with music, dancing, and celebration as residents

and tourists alike enjoy the colorful atmosphere.

Italy's festivals and festivities give a riveting peek into the country's rich cultural history, customs, and sense of community. Whether seeing ancient reenactments, feasting in regional cuisine, or partaking in colorful processions, experiencing Italy's vivid festivals is an amazing trip that celebrates the country's variety and long past.

- **Italian Lifestyle: The Art of Dolce Far Niente (Sweet Idleness)**

The Italian lifestyle is defined by a distinct concept known as "Dolce Far Niente," which translates to "sweet idleness" or "the sweetness of doing nothing." Rooted in the Italian culture's focus on leisure, enjoyment, and the appreciation of life's basic delights, Dolce Far Niente symbolizes a calm and leisurely attitude to living. Here's a comprehensive analysis of the Italian lifestyle and the art of Dolce Far Niente:

1. **Embracing Leisure**:

- In Italy, leisure is not considered as a luxury but as an integral element of everyday life. Italians emphasize spending time with family and friends, enjoying fine food and wine, and embracing moments of leisure. Whether it's lingering over a leisurely lunch at a trattoria, having an afternoon nap, or meandering around a piazza, Italians appreciate the importance of slowing down and savoring the present moment.

2. **Cultural Respect**:
- Italians have a great respect for art, music, literature, and history. From visiting world-renowned museums and art galleries to attending classical concerts and opera performances, Italians actively seek out cultural experiences that improve their lives and stimulate their creativity. The Italian culture inspires a love of beauty and a respect for the past, with many Italians taking delight in conserving and appreciating their cultural history.

3. **Epicurean Pleasures**:

- Central to Italian culture is a love of fine food and wine. Italians are enthusiastic about cooking and eating, and meals are a time for gathering, mingling, and indulging in great sensations. Whether it's sharing a traditional Sunday brunch with family, drinking an espresso at a sidewalk café, or tasting regional delicacies at a food festival, Italians take pleasure in the culinary pleasures of their rich gastronomic history.

4. **Community Connection**:
- Italians put significant significance on community and social relationships. Family reunions, neighborhood festivals, and local customs are vital components of Italian culture, generating a feeling of connection and togetherness. From the yearly grape harvest in remote villages to the colorful street festivals in busy metropolises, Italians gather together to celebrate common values, traditions, and experiences.

5. **Outdoor Enjoyment**:
- Italy's spectacular natural landscapes give numerous chances for outdoor enjoyment and relaxation. Whether it's lazing on a

sun-drenched beach along the Amalfi Coast, climbing in the rough mountains of the Dolomites, or touring stunning vineyards in Tuscany, Italians take full use of their country's natural beauty. Outdoor hobbies such as cycling, sailing, and gardening are valued pleasures that provide joy and satisfaction to everyday life.

6. **Balanced Living**:
- The Italian lifestyle stresses the necessity of balance and moderation in all things. While Italians adore leisure and pleasure, they also value health, well-being, and physical exercise. Daily rituals such as taking a passeggiata (evening promenade), practicing yoga, or playing a game of bocce allow chances to keep active and retain a feeling of well-being.

7. **Resilience and Adaptability**:
- Italians are famed for their perseverance and flexibility in the face of adversities. Throughout history, Italy has suffered times of political turbulence, economic hardship, and societal change, but Italians have always found ways to persist and prosper. The

Italian lifestyle encompasses a spirit of perseverance, optimism, and inventiveness that helps people negotiate life's ups and downs with grace and tenacity.

The Italian lifestyle is a celebration of leisure, pleasure, and the simple delights of daily existence. Rooted in the idea of Dolce Far Niente, Italians adopt a calm and leisurely attitude to life, appreciating each moment and finding beauty in the everyday. Whether having a leisurely lunch with loved ones, experiencing the great outdoors, or immersing oneself in cultural activities, Italians treasure the art of living well and finding satisfaction in the simple moments of life.

Chapter 6: Practical Travel Information

Traveling to Italy is an amazing trip packed with rich history, lively culture, and wonderful food. To guarantee a smooth and pleasurable journey, it's necessary to be prepared with practical travel knowledge. Here's a detailed resource to help you plan your journey:

- **Planning Your Trip: When to Go and What to Pack**

Planning a vacation to Italy includes considering aspects such as weather, people, and cultural events to ensure you have the best possible experience. Here's a thorough guide to help you select when to travel and what to bring for your Italian adventure:

1. **Choosing the Right Time to Visit**:
- Italy is a year-round destination, with each season presenting its own particular charms and attractions. The optimal time to visit

depends on your own choices, interests, and priorities.

- Peak tourist seasons in Italy are during the summer months of June, July, and August, when the weather is hot and sunny, and numerous attractions, beaches, and outdoor activities are in full flow. However, this is also when crowds are at their peak, prices are inflated, and popular places may be packed.

- Spring (April to May) and fall (September to October) are considered shoulder seasons in Italy, giving beautiful weather, fewer people, and reduced pricing. These seasons are perfect for tourism, outdoor activities, and attending cultural events and festivals.

- Winter (December to February) is the low season in Italy, with fewer visitors, lower weather, and the chance of rain or snow in some places. While certain sights and tourist services may have restricted hours or closures during this time, it's a terrific chance to explore Italy's cultural and culinary traditions, festive Christmas markets, and ski resorts in the Alps and Dolomites.

2. **Understanding Italian Weather**:

- Italy's climate varies from area to region, with the north having lower temperatures and the south enjoying warmer winters and hotter summers. Along the beaches and in southern parts, the Mediterranean climate offers mild, rainy winters and hot, dry summers, whereas interior areas and mountain regions have more continental climates with colder winters and warmer summers.

- Summer temperatures in Italy may skyrocket, particularly in southern and interior locations, with temperatures regularly topping 30°C (86°F). It's crucial to remain hydrated, use sunscreen, and seek shade during the warmest portions of the day.

- Spring and fall provide gentler temperatures and nice weather for outdoor activities, sightseeing, and seeing Italy's towns and countryside. Pack layers and adaptable clothes to meet shifting temperatures throughout the day.

3. **What to Pack**:

- **Clothes**: Pack lightweight, breathable clothes for summer months, like shorts, T-shirts, sundresses, and sandals. For spring and fall, include layers such as light sweaters, long-sleeved shirts, and a waterproof jacket or windbreaker. In winter, carry warm layers, including sweaters, jackets, scarves, gloves, and a waterproof jacket or coat.

- **Footwear**: Comfortable walking shoes are necessary for experiencing Italy's cobblestone streets, ancient attractions, and natural vistas. Opt for durable sneakers, comfy sandals, or walking shoes with sufficient support. If you want to visit churches or religious locations, pack closed-toe shoes to comply with dress rules.

- **Accessories**: Don't forget to take necessary accessories like sunglasses, a wide-brimmed hat or cap, sunscreen with high SPF, and a reusable water bottle to remain hydrated while exploring.

- **Documents and Essentials**: Carry vital travel papers such as your passport, visa (if necessary), travel insurance information, and copies of crucial documents kept securely in a travel wallet or pouch. Consider packing a universal converter and portable charger for your personal gadgets.

4. **Cultural Considerations**:

- When packing apparel for your vacation to Italy, consider local traditions and cultural standards. Italians prefer to dress stylishly and modestly, particularly in metropolitan areas and while visiting churches, cathedrals, and religious places. Avoid wearing exposing apparel, beachwear, or sports equipment in certain contexts.

- If you want to attend premium restaurants, theaters, or cultural events, carry smart-casual wear such as a dress shirt, blouse, or dress pants for men, and a dress, skirt, or formal trousers for women. A lightweight scarf or shawl may also be beneficial for concealing shoulders or adding a touch of refinement to your outfit.

5. **Special Considerations**:

- If you want to visit Italy during high tourist seasons or major events, consider reserving hotels, transportation, and excursions in advance to assure availability and prevent disappointment. Popular locations like Rome, Florence, and Venice might be extremely busy during these periods, so plan your trip appropriately.
- Pack a compact daypack or tote bag for carrying basics such as water, food, sunscreen, a map or guidebook, and any purchases or keepsakes you may accumulate throughout your travels. A lightweight, collapsible bag or backpack may also be ideal for day getaways, shopping excursions, or beach visits.

Preparing for your vacation to Italy entails considering aspects such as weather, people, and cultural events to guarantee a seamless and pleasurable experience. By picking the correct time to come, knowing Italian weather patterns, bringing suitable clothes and supplies, and being sensitive to cultural factors, you can make the most of your

Italian journey and create amazing memories in this lovely place.

- **Transportation: Getting Around Italy**

Italy features an extensive and efficient transportation network that makes it easier for tourists to experience its various landscapes, ancient cities, and beautiful towns. From high-speed trains and picturesque drives to ferries and local busses, here's a full guide to navigating around Italy:

1. **Trains**:
- Italy's national railway operator, Trenitalia, runs an extensive network of trains that link major cities, villages, and regions across the country. The high-speed rail service, called Frecciarossa (Red Arrow), enables rapid and pleasant travel between cities like as Rome, Milan, Florence, Venice, and Naples.
- Regional trains, such as the Frecciabianca (White Arrow) and Intercity, offer slower but cheaper choices for commuting between smaller towns and cities. These trains may

make many stops along the trip, making them excellent for visiting off-the-beaten-path places.

- It's important to book train tickets in advance, particularly for long-distance and high-speed lines, to get the greatest pricing and availability. Tickets may be bought online on the Trenitalia website, at train stations, or through approved ticket dealers.

2. **Busses**:

- In addition to trains, buses are a practical and economical choice for commuting throughout Italy, particularly in rural areas and places not serviced by rail. Bus companies such as FlixBus, MarinoBus, and Baltour provide routes linking major cities, villages, and tourist spots around the country.

- Local buses are an effective method to travel cities and towns, with complete networks covering metropolitan regions and suburban suburbs. Many cities also provide hop-on-hop-off tour buses that give easy transportation to major sites and landmarks.

3. **Metro and Trams**:

- Italy's largest cities, including Rome, Milan, Naples, Turin, and Florence, have efficient metro (subway) systems that allow rapid and comfortable transit within metropolitan regions. Metro lines are color-coded and simple to understand, with regular trains operating from early morning until late at night.

- Some cities, such as Milan and Rome, also have tram networks that supplement the metro system and give extra choices for moving about. Trams are a lovely and relaxing method to explore city streets and neighborhoods, with routes stretching to remote districts and suburbs.

4. **Ferries and Boats**:

- Italy's coastal areas and islands are readily accessible by ferry and boat, giving scenic trips and breathtaking views of the Mediterranean Sea. Ferry companies such as Tirrenia, Moby Lines, and Blu Navy provide services linking mainland Italy to places such as Sardinia, Sicily, Capri, and the Aeolian Islands.

- Ferries also offer transit between islands and coastal towns, with regular services operating throughout the day during the peak tourist season. It's essential to check boat timetables and buy tickets in advance, particularly for popular routes and peak travel hours.

5. **Vehicle Rentals**:

- Renting a vehicle is a popular alternative for visiting Italy's picturesque countryside, coastal areas, and medieval towns at your own speed. Major automobile rental firms such as Hertz, Avis, Europcar, and Sixt maintain offices at airports, rail stations, and city centers across Italy.

-Italy's well-maintained road network comprises highways (autostrade), regional roads (strade regional), and local roads (strade local), making it simple to drive between cities and attractions. However, driving in big cities may be problematic owing to traffic congestion, limited parking, and restricted driving zones (Zona a Traffico Limitato or ZTL).

6. **Cycling and Walking**:

- Italy's tiny towns, gorgeous countryside, and picturesque coastline locations are great for touring by bicycle or on foot. Many cities, like Florence, Venice, and Lucca, have dedicated bike lanes and pedestrian-friendly zones, making it safe and pleasurable to ride or stroll about.
- Bike-sharing schemes are offered in cities such as Rome, Milan, and Bologna, enabling tourists to borrow bicycles for short-term usage and explore local streets and attractions at their leisure. Guided walking tours are also common in historic city centers, giving insight into local culture, history, and architecture.

7. **Taxis and Ride-Sharing**:
- Taxis are frequently accessible in Italy's main cities and tourist destinations, offering convenient transportation for short distances or when public transit is not available. Licensed taxis are fitted with meters, and rates are controlled by municipal authorities.
- Ride-sharing services such as Uber, Lyft, and Bolt operate in certain cities throughout Italy, giving an alternative to conventional

taxis and public transit. These services are especially beneficial for going to and from airports, rail stations, and outlying areas not covered by public transportation.

8. **Planning and Tips**:
- Before going, acquaint yourself with Italy's transportation choices, timetables, and pricing structures to ensure a pleasant and efficient trip.
- Purchase tickets in advance for long-distance trains, buses, and ferries, particularly during busy tourist seasons and holidays, to assure availability and avoid lengthy lineups.
- Check the validity of your passport, driver's license, and any relevant visas or permits before renting a vehicle or driving in Italy. International driving permits (IDPs) are necessary for various nations.
- Be careful of local traditions, norms, and regulations while using public transit, such as giving up seats for elderly or handicapped people, verifying tickets before entering trains and buses, and following safety recommendations.

Italy provides a varied selection of transportation alternatives for tourists to see its dynamic cities, gorgeous landscapes, and cultural treasures. Whether going by rail, bus, boat, vehicle, or bike, preparing ahead and knowing the various alternatives can help you make the most of your vacation and create amazing moments in this lovely place.

- Accommodation Options: From Luxury Hotels to Agriturismi

Italy provides a broad assortment of hotel alternatives to meet any traveler's interests, price, and style. From opulent hotels and boutique bed-and-breakfasts to rustic agriturismo and quaint guesthouses, here's a thorough reference to the numerous housing alternatives available in Italy:

1. **Luxury Hotels**:
- Italy is home to some of the world's most prominent luxury hotels, providing unsurpassed comfort, elegance, and personalized service. These five-star

establishments are generally situated in ancient palaces, stately villas, and luxury resorts, with extravagant amenities such as spa facilities, gourmet restaurants, and panoramic views.

- Luxury hotel groups such as The Ritz-Carlton, Four Seasons, and Belmond operate facilities throughout Italy's main cities, seaside resorts, and rural estates, offering discriminating tourists with lavish rooms and immersive experiences.

2. **Boutique Hotels and Design Hotels**:
- Boutique hotels are tiny, individually owned businesses that provide beautiful lodgings, customized service, and distinctive design features. These tiny getaways generally offer unusual architecture, modern artwork, and elegant decor, providing a feeling of warmth and authenticity.

- Design hotels are defined by creative architecture, avant-garde décor, and cutting-edge services, appealing to guests with a love for contemporary design and innovation. Italy's main cities, such as Milan and Rome, are recognized for their thriving design hotel sector, with hotels that display the newest trends in architecture and interior design.

3. **Bed and Breakfasts (B&Bs)**:
- Bed and breakfasts are family-run enterprises that provide pleasant rooms and delicious meals in a relaxing, home-like setting. These lovely residences are generally situated in ancient houses, rural estates, and residential districts, giving tourists an insight into local life and culture.
- B&Bs vary in size and design, ranging from charming cottages and rustic farmhouses to luxurious townhouses and urban getaways. Many owners take delight in delivering customized hospitality and insider advice on area sights, restaurants, and activities.

4. **Agriturismi (Farm Stays)**:
- Agriturismi are functioning farms that provide lodging, eating, and recreational activities to tourists seeking a rural vacation and a genuine farm-to-table experience. These agrarian estates display Italy's agricultural history and traditional way of

life, encouraging tourists to engage in farm activities like harvesting, cheese-making, and wine-tasting.
- Agriturismi may be found across Italy's countryside, from the rolling hills of Tuscany and Umbria to the sun-drenched vineyards of Sicily and Puglia. Accommodations vary from basic bedrooms and flats to magnificent suites and private villas, generally surrounded by beautiful gardens, vineyards, and olive groves.

5. **Guesthouses and Pensioni**:
- Guesthouses, also known as pensioni, are family-operated lodgings that provide inexpensive lodging and minimal facilities to budget-conscious guests. These modest restaurants are generally situated in historic buildings, residential districts, and city centers, providing travelers with a pleasant and accessible base for visiting local sights and monuments.
- Guesthouses often provide individual rooms with shared or en-suite bathrooms, as well as communal amenities such as lounges, kitchens, and outside patios. Some

guesthouses may include breakfast in the accommodation fee, while others provide self-catering facilities for guests to cook their own meals.

6. Vacation Rentals and Apartments:

- Vacation rentals and apartments are popular alternatives for tourists wanting flexibility, freedom, and space during their time in Italy. These self-catering accommodations vary from studio apartments and city lofts to huge villas and rural cottages, giving visitors the comforts of home and the flexibility to explore at their own speed.

- Vacation rentals are available for short-term or long-term stays and are typically booked via internet platforms such as Airbnb, HomeAway, and Booking.com. They are great for families, parties, and tourists who like the privacy and convenience of having your own kitchen, living room, and outside space.

7. Hostels and Backpacker Accommodations:

- Hostels are budget-friendly lodgings that appeal to young travelers, backpackers, and budget-conscious explorers seeking economical accommodation and a convivial environment. These community residences include shared dormitory-style rooms, in addition to individual rooms and facilities such as common kitchens, lounges, and scheduled activities.
- Italy's main towns and tourist sites feature a broad range of hostels, ranging from raucous party hotels to laid-back eco-friendly hostels. They give a wonderful chance to meet other travelers, share travel advice, and immerse oneself in the backpacker lifestyle.

8. **Monasteries and Convents**:
- For guests seeking a unique and calm escape, monasteries and convents provide basic but serene lodgings in historic locations. These religious guesthouses accept guests of all religions and offer a calm space for thought, meditation, and spiritual renewal.

- Many monasteries and convents provide bedrooms with shared or private amenities, as well as communal spaces such as chapels, gardens, and libraries for visitors to explore and enjoy. Some facilities may serve communal meals or participate in local outreach projects, offering visitors with opportunity to interact with the community and enjoy a greater connection to their surroundings.

9. **Camping and Glamping:**
- For outdoor enthusiasts and nature lovers, camping and glamping (glamorous camping) provide a unique opportunity to appreciate Italy's natural beauties and picturesque landscapes. Campgrounds and campsites are spread across the country, from coastal beaches and lakeside getaways to alpine valleys and national parks.
- Camping amenities vary from simple tent pitches and RV sites to fully furnished cabins and safari tents, giving tourists alternatives for rustic or opulent camping experiences. Glamping lodgings frequently contain luxuries such as comfy mattresses,

en-suite bathrooms, and outside eating spaces, enabling visitors to experience the great outdoors without compromising comfort.

10. **Choosing the Right Accommodation**:
- When picking lodging in Italy, consider variables such as location, facilities, budget, and personal preferences. Research several possibilities and read reviews from prior visitors to guarantee a comfortable and happy stay.
- Think about the sort of experience you want to have during your vacation, whether it's resting in a luxury hotel, immersing yourself in local culture at a bed & breakfast, or connecting with nature at an agriturismo or campsite.
- Consider the closeness of your hotel to major attractions, public transit, restaurants, and other services. Choose a central location for convenience and easy access to surrounding landmarks, or go for a hidden hideaway for peace and solitude.
- Check for special offers, discounts, and package deals when reserving

accommodation, particularly during off-peak seasons or last-minute reservations. Many establishments offer specials such as early bird discounts, gratis upgrades, and comprehensive packages that combine accommodation with activities or eating experiences.

Italy provides a broad choice of housing alternatives to fit every traveler's requirements and interests, from opulent hotels and boutique bed-and-breakfasts to rustic agriturismo and beautiful guesthouses. Whether you're seeking a romantic retreat, a family-friendly escape, or an exciting outdoor adventure, there's something for everyone in Italy's varied accommodation environment. By selecting the proper lodging and preparing beforehand, you can make the most of your Italian experience and create amazing memories in this enchanting region.

- Budgeting Tips and Money Matters

Preparation for a trip to Italy includes careful budgeting and financial preparation to ensure that you get the most out of your vacation experience without overpaying. From planning a vacation budget and managing spending to locating economical hotels and dining alternatives, here's a thorough guide to budgeting ideas and money concerns in Italy:

1. **Setting a Travel Budget**:
- Before you start arranging your vacation, calculate how much you can afford to spend on transportation, housing, food, activities, and other expenditures. Consider aspects such as your travel style, length of stay, and desired degree of comfort when choosing your budget.
- Create a thorough budget spreadsheet or use a budgeting tool to log your costs and monitor your spending during your vacation. Allocate cash for basics like airfare, lodgings, and transportation, as well as

optional items such as eating out, shopping, and entertainment.

2. **Exchange Rates and Currency**:
- The official currency of Italy is the Euro (EUR), which is split into 100 cents (centesimi). Check the current exchange rates and conversion costs before converting currencies to guarantee you receive the greatest value for your money.
- Avoid exchanging money in airports, hotels, or tourist locations, as they frequently charge greater fees and give less advantageous exchange rates. Instead, utilize ATMs or currency exchange offices (cambio) situated in large cities and towns for better rates and reduced costs.

3. **Payment Methods**:
- Credit and debit cards are frequently accepted in Italy, particularly in large cities, tourist destinations, and upmarket restaurants. Visa and Mastercard are the most often accepted cards, followed by American Express and Discover.
- Notify your bank and credit card issuers of your trip intentions in advance to avoid your

cards from being stopped or reported for suspicious behavior while overseas. Be mindful of overseas transaction fees and currency translation costs that may apply to card transactions.

- Carry a modest quantity of cash for purchases at markets, street sellers, and smaller places that may not take cards. ATMs are widespread in Italy and enable you to withdraw cash in Euros using your debit or credit card.

4. **Budget-Friendly Lodgings**:

- Save money on lodgings by selecting budget-friendly choices such as hostels, guesthouses, bed and breakfasts, and vacation rentals. These alternatives frequently provide cheap prices, particularly during off-peak seasons or for extended stays.

- Consider vacationing in less popular places or suburbs outside big cities to discover inexpensive lodgings with convenient access to public transit. Booking hotels in advance may also help you acquire reduced prices and prevent last-minute price spikes.

5. **Eating on a Budget**:
- Dining out may be a huge expenditure when vacationing in Italy, but there are ways to enjoy wonderful meals without breaking the bank. Look for trattorias, osterias, and small cafés that offer inexpensive lunch specials (pranzo) or set menus (menu fisso) at fixed pricing.
- Take advantage of Italy's culinary culture by trying street cuisine, such as pizza al taglio (slice of pizza), panini (sandwiches), and arancini (stuffed rice balls), which are delectable and budget-friendly alternatives for fast meals on the move.
- Save money on eating expenditures by shopping at local markets and grocery shops for fresh vegetables, bread, cheese, and other supplies to cook your meals. Many places, particularly holiday rentals and flats, include kitchen facilities where you may cook basic meals and snacks.

6. **Transportation Savings**:
- Save money on transportation by adopting cost-effective solutions such as public buses, trams, and metro systems in big cities. Many

cities provide reduced multi-day tickets or tourist cards that enable unrestricted access to public transit and discounts on attractions.
- Consider obtaining a rail pass or regional train ticket for long-distance travel between cities and regions. Rail passes provide flexibility and cost savings for tourists wishing to visit many sites within a specified period.
- Make use of ride-sharing services, such as Uber, Lyft, and Bolt, for economical transportation inside cities or for short journeys to local sites. Sharing transportation with other passengers might help share costs and minimize expenditures.

7. **Free and Low-Cost Activities**:
- Explore Italy's cultural legacy and natural beauty without spending a lot by looking out for free or low-cost activities and attractions. Many museums, galleries, and historic sites provide free entry on particular days or during specified hours, so plan your trips appropriately.
- Enjoy outdoor activities like hiking, biking, and walking tours in Italy's

picturesque countryside, national parks, and coastal districts. Pack a picnic lunch and spend the day seeing quaint towns, historic castles, and stunning vistas.

- Attend local festivals, concerts, and cultural events to immerse yourself in Italy's thriving arts and entertainment scene. Look for neighborhood festivals, street performances, and religious festivities that give true cultural experiences at little to no expense.

8. **Tipping and Service Charges**:

- Tipping is not as prevalent or anticipated in Italy as it is in some other countries since service costs are generally included in the bill at restaurants, cafés, and pubs. Look for the words "servizio incluso" or "coperto" on the menu or receipt, which indicates that a service fee has been applied.

- While tipping is not necessary, it's traditional to round up the bill or give a little gratuity (about 5-10%) for excellent service, particularly in luxury restaurants or for extraordinary treatment. Consider tipping tour guides, drivers, and other service providers depending on the quality of service and your pleasure.

9. **Emergency Funds and Contingency Plans**:

- Be prepared for unforeseen costs and emergencies by putting away a part of your trip budget as an emergency fund. This fund may cover unanticipated expenditures such as medical crises, transportation delays, or lost or stolen belongings.

- Carry a backup credit card, debit card, or traveler's check in a different area from your main cards and cash. Store critical papers such as passport copies, travel insurance information, and emergency contact numbers in a secure area, such as a hotel safe or encrypted digital file.

10. **Cultural Sensitivity and Respect**:

- While it's crucial to keep to your budget and handle spending sensibly, remember to be respectful of local customs, traditions, and cultural norms. Avoid arguing over pricing or negotiating unduly, particularly in marketplaces, stores, and restaurants where prices are predetermined or non-negotiable.

- Support local companies, artists, and craftsmen by buying handcrafted souvenirs, artisanal items, and locally sourced goods. Patronize family-owned restaurants, cafés, and stores that highlight the finest of Italian food and workmanship.

Budgeting for a vacation to Italy includes careful preparation, ingenuity, and a willingness to select activities depending on your interests and economic limits. By creating a realistic trip budget, being conscious of expenditures, and making educated decisions regarding lodgings, food, transportation, and activities, you may have a wonderful and gratifying vacation experience in Italy without overpaying.

Remember to study and compare rates, take advantage of discounts and special offers, and seek out free or low-cost activities and attractions to optimize your savings while visiting Italy's rich cultural history, breathtaking landscapes, and dynamic towns. With careful preparation and smart budgeting, you can create wonderful experiences and make the most of your

Italian journey while keeping within your financial limits.

- **Safety and Health Considerations**

Traveling to Italy is an exciting and fascinating experience, but it's necessary to emphasize safety and health to guarantee a smooth and happy journey. From remaining safe in metropolitan areas to taking measures against common health concerns, here's a thorough reference to safety and health issues in Italy:

1. **General Safety Tips**:
- Italy is a generally secure nation for tourists, but it's vital to stay attentive and aware of your surroundings, particularly in popular tourist sites, public transit, and busy city streets.
- Keep your possessions safe and avoid carrying significant quantities of cash, valuables, or costly jewelry. Use a money belt, neck pouch, or anti-theft bag to hold your passport, money, credit cards, and other critical documents.

- Be aware of pickpockets and petty theft in busy locations like train stations, marketplaces, and tourist sites. Keep your bags closed, wallets in front pockets, and avoid exhibiting pricey electrical gadgets or cameras.
- Stay updated about local safety warnings, demonstrations, and protests that may affect travel plans. Follow advice from local authorities and avoid places where civil disturbance or political tensions are evident.

2. Transportation Safety:
- Use trustworthy and licensed transportation services, such as taxis, ride-sharing apps, and public transit, while going about cities and towns. Avoid unauthorized taxis and utilize official taxi stands or trustworthy firms suggested by your hotel.
- Exercise care while crossing roadways, particularly in major metropolitan locations where traffic may be fast-paced and unexpected. Look both ways before crossing, respect traffic lights, and utilize designated crosswalks where available.

- If hiring a vehicle, educate yourself with local driving rules, road signs, and restrictions. Italy has strong restrictions regulating speed limits, seat belt use, and alcohol intake while driving. Be wary of Zona a Traffico Limitato (ZTL) zones in city centers, where only approved cars are allowed.

3. **Health Precautions**:
- Italy has a high quality of healthcare and medical facilities, but it's vital to obtain travel insurance that covers medical bills, emergency evacuation, and repatriation in case of sickness or accident. Carry your insurance information and emergency contact numbers with you at all times.
- Ensure that regular immunizations are up-to-date before coming to Italy. Hepatitis A and B, influenza, and tetanus-diphtheria are recommended immunizations for travelers. Consult with your healthcare physician or travel clinic for specific recommendations depending on your health condition and vacation schedule.

- Pack a basic travel health kit containing vital drugs, over-the-counter treatments, and first-aid supplies for minor injuries and illnesses. Include goods like as pain medicines, antidiarrheal medication, antihistamines, bug repellant, sunscreen, and hand sanitizer.

- Practice excellent hygiene practices, such as washing your hands often with soap and water, particularly before eating, after using the toilet, and after touching surfaces in public spaces. Use alcohol-based hand sanitizer if soap and water are not available.

4. **Food and Water Safety**:

- Italian cuisine is known for its exquisite tastes and fresh ingredients, but it's vital to take care to avoid foodborne diseases. Eat at recognized restaurants, trattorias, and cafés that follow strict food hygiene and safety requirements.

- Avoid eating tap water unless it has been boiled, filtered, or treated with purification tablets. Stick to bottled water from trustworthy brands and avoid adding ice to

beverages unless it's prepared from filtered water.
- Be careful while ingesting raw or undercooked foods, such as shellfish, meat, eggs, and unpasteurized dairy products, since they may provide a risk of foodborne infections. Choose foods that are properly prepared and served scorching hot.

5. **Sun Protection**:
- Italy boasts a Mediterranean environment with scorching summers and ample sunlight, therefore it's vital to protect oneself from the sun's damaging rays. Wear sunscreen with a high SPF rating, broad-spectrum protection, and water resistance to avoid sunburn and skin damage.
- Seek shade during the warmest portion of the day, often between 10 a.m. and 4 p.m., and wear protective clothes such as lightweight long-sleeve shirts, wide-brimmed hats, and sunglasses with UV protection.

6. **Emergency Contacts**:
- Familiarize yourself with emergency contact numbers and procedures in Italy,

including the European emergency number 112, which enables access to police, fire, and medical services countrywide. Keep a list of vital contacts, including your lodging, embassy or consulate, and travel insurance provider.

7. **COVID-19 Precautions**:
- As of [current date], COVID-19 precautions and recommendations may still be in force in Italy. Stay updated on travel restrictions, entrance procedures, and health standards imposed by Italian authorities. Follow suggested precautions such as wearing masks in indoor public venues, adopting physical distance, and being vaccinated against COVID-19 before going.

Emphasizing safety and health issues is vital for a joyful and stress-free vacation experience in Italy. By being aware, taking measures, and maintaining good hygiene practices, you may reduce risks and enjoy everything that Italy has to offer while remaining safe and healthy during your visit.

- **Useful Phrases and Language Tips**

Navigating Italy is not only about enjoying the sights and tastes; it's also about engaging with people and immersing yourself in the lively culture. While English is frequently spoken in tourist regions, learning a few important Italian words will enrich your trip experience and help you communicate more successfully. Here's a full reference on important phrases and linguistic hints in Italy:

1. **Basic Greetings and Courtesy**:
- Buongiorno (BWON-jor-no) - Good morning
- Buonasera (BWOH-nah-seh-rah) - Good evening
- Buona notte (BWOH-nah NOH-teh) - Good night
- Ciao (chow) - Hello/Goodbye (informal)
- Salve (SAHL-veh) - Hello (formal)
- Grazie (GRAHT-see-eh) - Thank you
- Prego (PREH-goh) - You're welcome/Please
- Per favore (pair fah-VOH-reh) - Please

- Scusa (SKOO-zah) - Excuse me (informal)
- Mi scusi (mee SKOO-zee) - Excuse me (formal)
- Mi dispiace (mee dee-SPYAH-che) - I'm sorry

2. **Introductions and Politeness**:
- Come ti chiami? (KOH-meh tee KYAH-mee) - What's your name? (informal)
- Mi chiamo... (mee KYAH-moh) - My name is...
- Come sta? (KOH-meh stah) - How are you? (formal)
- Molto bene, grazie. E lei? (MOHL-toh BEH-neh, GRAHT-see-eh. Eh lay) - Very good, thank you. And you? (formal)
- Piacere di conoscerti. (pyah-CHEH-reh dee koh-noh-SHEHR-tee) - Nice to meet you. (informal)
- Piacere di conoscerla. (pyah-CHEH-reh dee koh-noh-SHEHR-lah) - Nice to meet you. (formal)

3. **Asking for Help and Directions**:
- Parla inglese? (PAHR-lah een-GLEH-zeh)
- Do you speak English?

- Posso aiutarla? (POHS-soh eye-oo-TAHR-lah) - Can I assist you? (formal)
- Dov'è...? (doh-VEH) - Where is...?
- Quanto costa? (KWAN-toh KOH-stah) - How much does it cost?
- Posso avere il conto, per favore? (POHS-soh ah-VEH-reh eel KOHN-toh, pair fah-VOH-reh) - Can I have the bill, please?

4. **Ordering Food and Drinks**:
- Vorrei... (vohr-RAY) - I would want...
- Un caffè, per favore. (oon kah-FEH, pair fah-VOH-reh) - A coffee, please.
- Un bicchiere di vino rosso/bianco, per favore. (oon BEEK-kyeh-reh dee VEE-noh ROSS-oh/BYAHN-koh, pair fah-VOH-reh) - A glass of red/white wine, please.
- Il conto, per favore. (eel KOHN-toh, pair fah-VOH-reh) - The bill, please.
- Cosa mi consiglia? (KO-sah mee kohn-SEELY-yah) - What do you recommend?

5. **Shopping and Bargaining**:

- Quanto costa questo? (KWAN-toh KOH-stah KWEH-stoh) - How much does this cost?

- Posso pagare con carta di credito? (POHS-soh pah-GAH-reh kohn KAR-tah dee KREH-dee-toh) - Can I pay with a credit card?

- Posso avere uno sconto? (POHS-soh ah-VEH-reh OO-noh SKOHN-toh) - Can I have a discount?

- Va bene. (vah BEH-neh) - That's fine/Okay.

- Troppo caro! (TROHP-poh KAH-roh) - Too pricey!

6. **Emergency Situations**:

- Aiuto! (ah-YOO-toh) - Help!

- Chiami un'ambulanza! (KYAH-mee oon am-boo-LAHN-zah) - Call an ambulance!

- Ho bisogno di un doctor. (oh bee-ZOH-nyoh dee soon MEH-dee-koh) - I need a doctor.

- Sono perso/a. (SOH-noh PEHR-soh/ah) - I'm lost. (male/female)

- Ho perso il mio passaporto. (oh PEHR-soh eel MEE-oh pah-sah-POHR-toh) - I've misplaced my passport.
- C'è stato un incidente. (cheh STAH-toh oon een-CHEE-den-teh) - There's been an accident.
- Dov'è il bagno? (doh-VEH eel BAH-nyoh) - Where is the bathroom?

7. **Cultural Etiquette**:
- When welcoming someone, it's traditional to shake hands, particularly in formal contexts. Kissing on the cheek (a kiss on each cheek) is customary among friends and relatives.
- Use formal language (lei) when addressing strangers, seniors, or those in positions of power. Informal language (tu) is used among friends, classmates, and children. - Italians cherish politeness and respect, so remember to say "please" (per favorite) and "thank you" (grazie) regularly.
- Dress modestly while visiting churches, religious places, and formal institutions. Cover your shoulders and knees, and avoid wearing exposed attire.

- Tipping is not mandatory in Italy, since a service fee (servizio incluso) is sometimes included in the bill. However, rounding up the amount or giving a little tip for great service is appreciated.

8. **Language Learning Tips**:
- Practice basic Italian phrases and vocabulary before your travel utilizing language learning apps, online resources, or language classes. Focus on important terms linked to travel, eating, shopping, and emergency.

- Immerse yourself in the language by listening to Italian music, viewing Italian films or TV programs, and practicing with native speakers if feasible. Try to engage in interactions with locals throughout your travels.

- Don't be scared to make errors while speaking Italian. Locals appreciate the effort and will frequently be patient and sympathetic, even if your language abilities are weak.

- Carry a pocket-sized phrasebook or download a language translation app on your smartphone for fast reference and help when required. Practice pronunciation and intonation to enhance your speaking abilities.

By learning a few basic words and embracing the Italian language and culture, you can enrich your travel experience, interact with people on a deeper level, and make wonderful memories throughout your stay in Italy. Whether you're purchasing a cappuccino at a café, asking for directions to a renowned site, or starting up a discussion with a friendly local, knowing a little of Italian can enhance your travel and make your stay more pleasurable.

Chapter 7: Insider Tips and Recommendations

Italy is a dream destination for many people because of its extensive history, breathtaking scenery, and gastronomic pleasures that are unmatched by any other country. It is important to take into consideration the following insider tips and ideas from both experienced visitors and locals to get the most out of your trip to Italy:

- Off-the-Beaten-Path Destinations

Italy is home to a multitude of hidden jewels and lesser-known places that are just waiting to be discovered, even though famous towns such as Rome, Florence, and Venice draw millions of travelers every year. The following are some off-the-beaten-path sites in Italy that promise to provide experiences that will be unforgettable: quaint medieval towns, pure natural landscapes, and picturesque natural settings.

1. **In the region of Matera, Basilicata**: The city of Matera, often known as the "City of Stones," is well-known for the ancient cave houses, also known as Sassi, that have been cut into the harsh topography. As you make your way through the winding alleyways of this UNESCO World Heritage site, see the spectacular views of the ravine below, and explore among the old chapels and cave churches that are scattered throughout the area.
2. **Alberobello, located in Puglia**: - Step into a magical world at Alberobello, where you'll discover a unique landscape filled with hundreds of trulli, rustic stone houses with conical roofs. Explore the small alleyways of this UNESCO-listed town, visit the Trullo Sovrano museum, and immerse yourself in the local culture and food.
3. **Sperlonga, Lazio**: Get away from the throng and take in the breathtaking scenery of Sperlonga, a charming seaside hamlet that is located between Rome and Naples. Relax on gorgeous beaches, visit the ancient remains of the Villa of Tiberius, and

meander through the picturesque alleyways of the old town.

4. **Orvieto, Umbria**: - Perched above a volcanic plateau, Orvieto is a medieval hilltop town noted for its beautiful Duomo, complex paintings, and labyrinthine subterranean passageways. Take a guided tour of the Orvieto Underground, drink local wines at family-owned vineyards, and experience panoramic views of the Umbrian countryside.

5. **Cinque Terre, Liguria (Less-Visited Trails)**: - While the Cinque Terre towns are famous tourist sites, travel off the main route to discover lesser-known hiking paths and quiet coves. Discover hidden jewels like Corniglia's terraced vineyards, the ancient town of Volastra, and the craggy coastline of the Portovenere Regional Park.

6. **Bologna, Emilia-Romagna (Hidden Courtyards and Markets)**: - Dive into the lively food scene and hidden wonders of Bologna, Italy's gastronomic capital. Explore the city's network of secret courtyards (cortili) and hidden alleyways

(vicoli), shop local markets like Mercato delle Erbe and Mercato di Mezzo, and sample classic specialties like tortellini en brodo and tagliatelle al ragù.

7. **Ragusa, Sicily**: - Lose yourself in the Baroque grandeur of Ragusa, a UNESCO-listed town in southern Sicily. Explore the old heart of Ragusa Ibla, meander down cobblestone alleyways lined with majestic palaces and churches, and enjoy Sicilian food in trattorias and cafés nestled away in secluded piazzas.

8. **Civita di Bagnoregio, Lazio**: - Discover the "Dying Town" of Civita di Bagnoregio, built on a crumbling tufa hill in the Tuscia area of Lazio. Cross the footbridge to this historic settlement, appreciate its medieval architecture, and absorb the magnificent views of the surrounding valley.

9. **Valle d'Aosta:** - Escape to the unspoiled wilderness of Valle d'Aosta, a mountainous area in northern Italy noted for its rocky peaks, alpine meadows, and lovely towns. Explore the medieval castles of Fénis and Issogne, walk through the Gran Paradiso

National Park, and try local delicacies like fontina cheese and lardo di Arnad.

10. **Molise**: - Experience the pristine beauty of Molise, one of Italy's least-visited areas, tucked between the Apennine Mountains and the Adriatic Sea. Explore ancient hilltop villages like Campobasso and Termoli, trek through the Matese Regional Park, and rest on the beautiful beaches of the Costa dei Trabocchi.

Italy is full of hidden gems and off-the-beaten-path locations waiting to be found. Whether you're discovering ancient cave homes in Matera, trekking along lonely paths in the Cinque Terre, or eating Sicilian food in Ragusa, these lesser-known jewels give a look into Italy's rich history, culture, and natural beauty away from the masses. Venture off the main road and find the hidden gems of Italy for a really unique vacation.

- Hidden Gems and Local Favorites

Italy is a country rich with recognized buildings and iconic locations, yet some of its most charming secrets lie off the main path. From secret jewels adored by locals to lesser-known places waiting to be found, here are some hidden gems and local favorites in Italy:

1. **San Leo, Emilia-Romagna**:
- Tucked hidden amid the rolling hills of Emilia-Romagna, the ancient town of San Leo gives a look into Italy's rich history and breathtaking vistas. Explore the majestic stronghold, set on a rocky outcrop overlooking the Marecchia Valley, and meander through tiny cobblestone lanes dotted with quaint cafés and artisan stores.

2. **Castelmezzano and Pietrapertosa, Basilicata**:
- Nestled in the steep landscape of the Lucanian Dolomites, Castelmezzano and Pietrapertosa are two charming towns linked by the "Flight of the Angel" zipline. Take in spectacular views of the surrounding

mountains, see old churches and stone buildings, and sample local specialties like lucanica sausage and pepperoni crushing (sun-dried peppers).

3. Monte Isola, Lombardy:
- Floating serenely on Lake Iseo, Monte Isola is one of Italy's best-kept secrets. Explore the car-free island by foot or bicycle, meander through small fishing towns like Peschiera Maraglio and Sensole, and trek to the Sanctuary of Madonna della Ceriola for panoramic views of the lake and surrounding mountains.

4. Procida, Campania:
- Escape the masses of Capri and Amalfi and explore the colorful beauty of Procida, a hidden jewel in the Bay of Naples. Stroll around meandering alleyways lined with pastel-hued buildings, sunbathe on scenic beaches like Marina di Corricella and Chiaiolella, and eat delicious seafood at waterfront trattorias.

5. Spello, Umbria:
- Known as the "flower town" of Umbria, Spello captivates tourists with its

blossoming flower displays, medieval architecture, and panoramic views of the Umbrian landscape. Explore ancient Roman ruins, meander through fragrant flower-lined lanes, and see works by Pinturicchio and Perugino in the town's churches and museums.

6. **Castelluccio di Norcia, Umbria**:
- Perched on a slope in the Sibillini Mountains, Castelluccio di Norcia is noted for its vivid flower fields, notably during the annual "Fioritura" in late April. Hike through the gorgeous countryside, consume local delicacies like lentils and cured meats, and relish stunning views of the Piano Grande.

7. **Matera, Basilicata (Beyond the Sassi)**:
- While Matera's Sassi districts are well-known, explore beyond the UNESCO-listed caverns to uncover hidden treasures like the Murgia Materana Park. Explore historic rock churches, stroll along magnificent paths overlooking the Gravina Canyon, and visit the Casa Grotta di Vico

Solitario to experience life in a typical cave home.

8. **Gubbio, Umbria**:
- Step back in time in the historic village of Gubbio, nestled on the slopes of Mount Ingino in Umbria. Explore ancient monuments like the Palazzo dei Consoli and the Roman Theater, ride the funicular to the Basilica of Saint Ubaldo, and participate in the annual Corsa dei Ceri festival, a centuries-old tradition.

9. **Pitigliano, Tuscany**:
- Known as the "Little Jerusalem" of Tuscany, Pitigliano is a lovely hilltop hamlet with a significant Jewish tradition. Wander through small alleyways and tunnels cut into tufa rock, explore the historic Jewish ghetto and synagogue, and enjoy local delicacies like acquacotta soup and wild boar ragù.

10. **Atrani, Campania (Amalfi Coast's Hidden Gem)**:
- Escape the throng of the Amalfi Coast and experience the beauty of Atrani, a little fishing hamlet located between Amalfi and Minori. Stroll around small alleyways and

pastel-colored cottages, sunbathe on the beach at Piazza Umberto I, and eat classic Neapolitan meals at family-run trattorias. Italy's hidden jewels and local favorites give an insight into the country's various landscapes, rich history, and lively culture. Whether you're seeing historic hilltop villages in Umbria, meandering through flower-filled fields in Umbria, or soaking up the sun on a quiet beach in Campania, these lesser-known sites guarantee amazing experiences and memories to last a lifetime. Venture off the main road and find the hidden beauties of Italy for a genuinely authentic and engaging travel experience.

- **Must-Try Dishes and Restaurants**

Italian food is known globally for its rich tastes, fresh ingredients, and regional delicacies. From exquisite pasta meals to delectable seafood, here are five must-try foods and places in Italy that guarantee to excite your taste buds and fulfill your gastronomic cravings:

1. **Pizza Margherita - Naples, Campania**:
- No vacation to Italy is complete without indulging in a genuine Neapolitan pizza. Head to Pizzeria Brandi in Naples, where the famed Pizza Margherita was originally produced in 1889 to commemorate Queen Margherita of Savoy. Made with San Marzano tomatoes, fresh mozzarella, basil, and extra-virgin olive oil, this simple but delectable pizza is a real Italian masterpiece.

2. **Risotto alla Milanese - Milan, Lombardy**:
- Sample the thick and creamy Risotto alla Milanese at Trattoria Masuelli San Marco in Milan. This classic meal is cooked with Arborio rice, saffron, butter, and Parmigiano-Reggiano cheese, resulting in a rich risotto with a vivid yellow color and delicate taste.

3. **Pasta all'Amatriciana - Rome, Lazio**:
- Savor the original tastes of Pasta all'Amatriciana at Trattoria da Cesare al Casaletto in Rome. This classic Roman meal comprises bucatini pasta mixed in a savory sauce prepared with guanciale (cured pig

cheek), tomatoes, pecorino cheese, and a dash of chili pepper for a bit of spice.

4. **Tagliatelle al Ragu - Bologna, Emilia-Romagna**:
- Treat yourself to a plate of Tagliatelle al Ragu at Trattoria Anna Maria in Bologna, the origin of this famous pasta dish. Made with fresh egg pasta ribbons and a rich beef sauce cooked for hours, this Bolognese dish is the essence of comfort food.

5. **Linguine alle Vongole - Naples, Campania**:
- Head to Trattoria da Nennella in Naples to experience Linguine alle Vongole, a famous seafood pasta dish comprising linguine noodles mixed with fresh clams, garlic, white wine, parsley, and a drizzle of extra-virgin olive oil. Pair it with a glass of fresh Falanghina wine for the ultimate supper.

6. **Cacio e Pepe - Rome, Lazio**:
- Indulge in the simple but delicious tastes of Cacio e Pepe at Roscioli in Rome. This famous Roman pasta dish is created with spaghetti or tonnarelli pasta, Pecorino

Romano cheese, black pepper, and a dash of pasta boiling water to make a creamy sauce that coats every strand of pasta.

7. Fritto Misto di Mare - Venice, Veneto:
- Delight in the tastes of the sea with Fritto Misto di Mare at Osteria Bancogiro in Venice. This Venetian delicacy contains a crispy mix of fried seafood, including shrimp, calamari, and tiny fish, served with a squeeze of lemon and a sprinkling of sea salt.

8. Osso Buco - Milan, Lombardy:
- Treat yourself to Osso Buco at Trattoria del Nuovo Macello in Milan, a substantial Milanese meal with braised veal shanks cooked in a rich tomato-based sauce with carrots, celery, onions, and gremolata (a zesty garnish prepared with lemon zest, garlic, and parsley). Pair it with creamy saffron risotto for a very fulfilling supper.

9. Panzanella - Florence, Tuscany:
- Enjoy the refreshing tastes of Panzanella at Osteria All'Antico Vinaio in Florence. This Tuscan bread salad is created with stale bread, ripe tomatoes, cucumber, red onion,

basil, and a drizzle of extra-virgin olive oil and vinegar, making it the ideal meal to enjoy on a hot summer day.

10. **Gelato - Throughout Italy**:
- Indulge your sweet craving with handcrafted gelato from Gelateria dei Gracchi in Rome. With a vast assortment of flavors crafted with fresh seasonal ingredients, including creamy pistachio, aromatic strawberry, and delicious chocolate, Gelateria dei Gracchi is a favorite among residents and tourists alike.

Italy's culinary landscape is a feast for the senses, with a variety of must-try dishes and places waiting to be discovered. Whether you're indulging in pizza in Naples, spaghetti in Rome, or gelato in Florence, each mouthful delivers a flavor of Italy's rich culinary tradition and enthusiasm for delicious cuisine. So, immerse yourself in the tastes of Italy and go on a culinary trip that will satisfy your tongue and leave you yearning more. Buon appetito!

- **Cultural Etiquette and Customs**

Italy is a nation rich in history, art, and culture, and its customs and etiquette reflect its deep-rooted traditions and ideals. Understanding and respecting Italian cultural standards will enrich your experience and help you navigate social interactions with ease. Here are some significant features of cultural etiquette and traditions in Italy:

1. **Greeting Etiquette**:
- When meeting someone for the first time, it is usual to greet them with a handshake and establish eye contact. In more casual circumstances, close friends and relatives may exchange kisses on the cheek, first with the left cheek and then the right.

 - Address individuals using their titles and last names, particularly in formal situations or when speaking to elders or persons in positions of power. Use "Signore" (Mr.) or "Signora" (Mrs.) followed by the person's last name.

2. **Politeness and Respect**:

- Italians put considerable significance on politeness and respect in social interactions. Always use "please" (per favor) and "thank you" (grazie) when making requests or expressing thanks.
- Show respect for seniors by addressing them with formal language (lei) and utilizing titles such as "Signora" or "Signor" followed by their last name. Avoid utilizing familiar language (tu) until requested to do so.

3. **Dining Etiquette**:
- Meals are a key aspect of Italian culture, and eating etiquette is treated seriously. Wait to be seated by the host and wait for everyone to be served before beginning your meal.
- It is usual to have your hands visible on the table while eating, with your wrists resting on the edge. Avoid resting your elbows on the table, since this is considered impolite.
- When completed eating, arrange your utensils parallel to each other on the plate with the tips toward the correct side. Do not cross them, since this signals that you are still eating.

4. **Dress Code**:
- Italians take pleasure in their appearance and wearing properly is vital, particularly in formal situations. When attending churches, museums, or fine restaurants, dress modestly and avoid wearing shorts, tank tops, or beachwear.
- In more informal situations, such as cafés or outdoor markets, comfortable and elegant apparel is allowed. However, avoid extremely exposing or flamboyant apparel, since this may be considered improper.

5. **Punctuality**:
- While Italians are renowned for their easygoing attitude to time, punctuality is nevertheless prized in professional and formal contexts. Arrive on time for appointments, meetings, and social gatherings, but be prepared for some flexibility in schedule.

6. **Cultural Sensitivity**:
- Respect cultural differences and avoid sensitive themes such as politics or religion until requested to discuss them. Refrain from expressing derogatory remarks about

Italy or its culture, since this may be considered insulting.

- Be conscious of local customs and traditions, particularly in rural regions or tiny villages. Take cues from locals and follow their example in social settings to avoid unwittingly causing offense.

7. **Tipping Etiquette**:

- Tipping is not as customary in Italy as it is in some other countries, since a service fee (coperto) is sometimes included in the bill. However, giving a modest gratuity for good service is appreciated, particularly in tourist destinations or luxury places.

8. **Greetings and Farewells**:

- When entering a business or restaurant, it is appropriate to greet the workers with a courteous "Buongiorno" (good morning) or "Buona sera" (good evening). Similarly, while departing, say "arrivederci" (goodbye) or "ciao" (casual goodbye) to bid farewell.

By familiarizing yourself with these cultural etiquette and customs in Italy, you may show respect for local traditions and beliefs while enjoying unique experiences and creating important relationships with the people you encounter. Embrace the Italian way of life and immerse yourself in the rich cultural fabric of this wonderful nation.

- **Sustainable Travel Practices**

As the tourist industry continues to develop, it becomes more necessary to embrace sustainable travel practices to reduce environmental effects, protect cultural heritage, and assist local communities. Italy, with its rich history, magnificent landscapes, and dynamic culture, provides several choices for sustainable travel. Here are some thorough, extensive, and complete sustainable travel practices to consider while touring Italy:

1. **Choose Eco-Friendly Accommodation**:
- Opt for lodgings that promote sustainability, such as eco-friendly hotels, bed and breakfasts, or agriturismi (farm stays). Look for places with green certifications, energy-efficient practices,

trash reduction programs, and locally produced amenities.

2. **Reduce Carbon Footprint**:

- Minimize your carbon footprint by using ecologically friendly ways of transportation. Utilize public transit, such as trains, buses, and trams, wherever feasible. Consider renting hybrid or electric automobiles for longer excursions, or explore cities on foot or by bicycle to cut emissions.

3. **Support Sustainable Tourism Initiatives**:

- Seek tour operators, guides, and experiences that encourage responsible tourism practices and sustainable development. Choose eco-friendly trips that concentrate on cultural immersion, animal conservation, or community participation, and support local businesses and craftsmen.

4. **Conserve Water and Energy**:

- Practice water and energy conservation throughout your stay in Italy. Take shorter showers, switch off lights and appliances when not in use, and reuse towels and linens to save water and energy use at hotels and motels.

5. **Respect Natural and Cultural Heritage**:
- Respect natural environments, animals, and cultural heritage places throughout your travels in Italy. Stay on established paths, avoid disturbing animals, and abstain from touching or removing antiquities or historical items. Observe local customs, traditions, and etiquette to demonstrate respect for Italy's cultural history.

6. **Reduce Single-Use Plastics:**
- Minimize plastic waste by eliminating single-use plastics, such as water bottles, straws, and plastic bags. Carry a reusable water bottle and replenish it at water fountains or filtered water stations. Bring reusable shopping bags and containers for souvenirs and food.

7. **Support Sustainable Dining**:
- Choose restaurants and cafes that stress sustainability by acquiring local, organic, and seasonal foods. Look for restaurants that promote fair trade practices, prevent food waste, and provide vegetarian or plant-based

menu alternatives. Support farmers' markets, food cooperatives, and Slow Food projects to support sustainable agricultural and culinary traditions.

8. **Practice Responsible Animal Tourism**:
- Avoid activities that exploit or hurt animals, such as captive animal attractions or wildlife selfies. Instead, seek out ethical wildlife activities, such as birding, whale watching, or nature walks conducted by qualified guides that stress animal care and conservation.

9. **Dispose of Waste Properly**:
- Dispose of waste responsibly by recycling, composting, and properly disposing of litter. Follow local recycling standards and utilize designated recycling containers for paper, plastic, glass, and organic garbage. Avoid littering in natural places and bring away any garbage you make during outdoor activities.

10. **Educate Yourself and Others**:
- Educate yourself on sustainability problems and best practices for ethical tourism in Italy. Share your knowledge and

experiences with others to create awareness and support positive behavior change. Support educational programs, conservation projects, and environmental groups fighting to safeguard Italy's natural and cultural legacy.

By adopting sustainable travel habits in Italy, you can limit your environmental imprint, assist local communities, and help the preservation of Italy's natural beauty and cultural history for future generations to enjoy. Together, we can develop a more sustainable and ethical tourism business that benefits both passengers and destinations alike.

Sicilia, Italia

Conclusion

"The Ultimate Guide to Italy: From Alps to the Apennines" by David A. Davidson provides readers a thorough and engaging trip through the various landscapes, rich history, and lively culture of Italy. From the beautiful peaks of the Alps to the rolling valleys of the Apennines, this handbook gives in-depth insights, practical guidance, and insider secrets to help tourists make the most of their Italian journey.

Throughout the book, readers are given thorough descriptions of Italy's renowned sites, hidden jewels, and off-the-beaten-path places. From the busy streets of Rome to the peaceful coasts of Sicily, each chapter is thoroughly researched and lovingly produced to present readers with a greater knowledge of Italy's diverse personality.

One of the book's major aspects is its focus on sustainability and ethical travel practices. By showcasing eco-friendly lodgings, supporting local businesses, and advocating cultural conservation, the book encourages readers to travel ethically and limit their environmental effects.

Moreover, "The Ultimate Guide to Italy" goes beyond standard guidebooks by digging into the complexities of Italian culture, etiquette, and traditions. Through informative commentary and practical recommendations, readers develop a better appreciation for the customs, food, and lifestyle that constitute Italy's distinctive personality.

Whether planning a first-time visit or trying to explore hidden gems, readers of "The Ultimate Guide to Italy" will find inspiration and assistance to create memorable experiences in this enchanting nation. With its thorough coverage, engaging writing style, and dedication to sustainability, this book is an excellent companion for anybody eager to see Italy's various landscapes and timeless charms.

Bonus

- 3 budget-friendly restaurants in Italy

1. **Trattoria da Michele - Naples, Campania**:
- Located in the center of Naples, Trattoria da Michele is a treasured institution recognized for its inexpensive and genuine Neapolitan food. Featured in the film "Eat Pray Love," this family-run trattoria has been dishing up traditional cuisine since 1870. Visitors come to Trattoria da Michele for its famed Margherita and Marinara pizzas, produced with fresh ingredients and cooked in a wood-fired oven. The menu also offers traditional pasta dishes like spaghetti alle vongole (clam pasta) and gnocchi alla sorrentina (potato dumplings with tomato and mozzarella). With its relaxed ambiance and wallet-friendly costs, Trattoria da Michele is a must-visit for budget-conscious tourists seeking a genuine flavor of Naples.

2. **Osteria del Cinghiale Bianco - Florence, Tuscany**:

- Nestled in the old Oltrarno area of Florence, Osteria del Cinghiale Bianco is a delightful trattoria famed for its cheap Tuscan food and comfortable setting. The restaurant focuses on robust cuisine produced with locally obtained ingredients, including wild boar (cinghiale), a regional specialty. Guests may savor Tuscan staples including pappa al pomodoro (tomato and bread soup), ribollita (Tuscan bean soup), and tagliatelle al ragù di cinghiale (wild boar ragù pasta). With its low rates and pleasant service, Osteria del Cinghiale Bianco delivers a taste of classic Tuscan food without breaking the budget.

3. **Cantina Do Spade - Venice, Veneto**:
- Situated in the historic center of Venice, Cantina Do Spade is a typical osteria that has been feeding hungry tourists since 1448. This centuries-old institution serves a selection of modest but tasty Venetian meals at budget-friendly pricing. Visitors may try local delicacies such as Cicchetti (small nibbles), bacalà mantecato (creamed fish), and sarde in saor (sweet and sour sardines).

The Osteria also provides a range of inexpensive wines including prosecco, great for mixing with Venetian Cicchetti. With its rustic setting and historic charm, Cantina Do Spade gives a genuine dining experience in the center of Venice at a reasonable rate. Overall, these budget-friendly restaurants in Italy provide tourists the chance to sample wonderful regional food without overpaying. Whether relishing Neapolitan pizza in Naples, Tuscan classics in Florence, or Venetian Cicchetti in Venice, tourists may indulge in Italy's gastronomic pleasures without breaking the budget.

Budget-friendly hotels in the top 3 cities

Italy's most important cities are well-known for their extensive histories, cultural sites, and lively atmospheres, all of which draw tourists from all over the globe. Travelers who prioritize their financial well-being and aim to explore these renowned destinations affordably will discover a diverse range of budget-friendly options available. A comprehensive and in-depth look at hotels that are beneficial to one's wallet in Italy's top three cities is as follows:

1. **Rome**:

Hotel des Artistes: Located conveniently near Rome's Termini Station, Hotel Des Artistes offers accommodations that are kind to one's wallet in the very center of the city. The hotel offers rooms that are not only pleasant but also equipped with contemporary conveniences such as free Wi-Fi and air conditioning. Every morning, guests have the chance to enjoy a complimentary continental breakfast before setting out to explore Rome's attractions. attractions, which include the Colosseum, Roman Forum, and Trevi Fountain.

Paba Hotel: [Hotel Paba] Situated in the lovely area of Trastevere, Hotel Paba offers economical accommodation in a gorgeous location. The hotel's rooms are comfortablhistoricale furthermore, the rooms feature private bathrooms and satellite television. Additionally, select rooms offer views of the Basilica of Basi Santa Maria in Trastevere, which is located nearby. Guests may walk the cobblestone alleyways of Trastevere, eat genuine Roman food at local trattorias, and conveniently reach the city's main attractions via adjacent tram and bus stations.

2. **Florence**:

Hotel Bretagna: Conveniently situated near Florence's Santa Maria Novella Station, Hotel Bretagna provides budget-friendly lodgings within walking distance of the city's major attractions. The hotel's modest rooms include traditional design and basic facilities, including free Wi-Fi and flat-screen TVs. Guests may start their day with a continental breakfast buffet before experiencing Florence's Renaissance architecture, world-class museums, and renowned monuments like the Duomo and Ponte Vecchio.

Hotel Nuova Italia: Nestled in the historic city of Florence, Hotel Nuova Italia offers economical accommodation in a good position. The hotel's modest rooms feature comfy mattresses and en-suite bathrooms, with some boasting views of the surrounding San Lorenzo Market. Guests may drink up the ambiance of Florence's busy streets, admire masterpieces at the Uffizi Gallery, and sample traditional Tuscan meals at neighboring trattorias and osterias.

3. **Venice**:

Hotel Guerrini: Situated near Venice's Santa Lucia Train Station, Hotel Guerrini provides budget-friendly lodgings in the city's historic Cannaregio area. The hotel's charming rooms include Venetian-style décor and contemporary amenities, like complimentary Wi-Fi and flat-screen TVs. Guests may explore Venice's picturesque streets and canals, see renowned monuments like St. Mark's Square and the Rialto Bridge, and indulge in Cicchetti (Venetian tapas) at local bacari (wine bars).

Hotel Marte: Located in the Cannaregio district, Hotel Marte offers economical accommodation in a tranquil residential location away from the throng. The hotel's basic rooms provide private bathrooms and minimal decor, with some overlooking the neighboring canals. Guests may escape the tourist hordes and explore hidden jewels in Venice, such as the Jewish Ghetto and the calm islands of Murano and Burano.

Budget-friendly hotels in Italy's best cities give guests decent lodgings, handy locations, and easy access to the city's key attractions. Whether visiting the ancient ruins of Rome, admiring Renaissance art in Florence, or navigating the labyrinthine canals of Venice, these modest hotel choices give the ideal foundation for budget-conscious visitors to enjoy the beauty of Italy's most renowned cities.

Printed in Great Britain
by Amazon